THEODORE LEVITT
is professor of business administration at
Harvard University. He received his doc-
toral degree from Ohio State University
and has authored numerous books and
articles on business subjects, for which
he has won five McKinsey Awards, and
most recently the John Hancock Award.

THE
THIRD SECTOR

THE
THIRD SECTOR

New Tactics
for a Responsive Society

THEODORE LEVITT

A DIVISION OF AMERICAN MANAGEMENT ASSOCIATIONS

FOREWORD

CONTRADICTORILY, a "foreword" is an afterthought, written when all else is done. It gives the author an opportunity to explain his reasons for writing the book he has just written, and—more self-indulgently—it gives him an opportunity to say a few words to people he knows personally.

In earlier days I wrote a good deal on social matters; more recently I have been writing on matters of business administration. The two are not unrelated, though the less informed feel that no one can be wise and objective about social issues if he has any contaminating familiarity with how the business of administration actually works in the world. My interest in business grew out of the early realization that economic organizations are the central institutions of all societies, even those that make a ritual show of denying that inescapable reality. Other powerful institutions and influences reign everywhere. Among these is an unavoidable relationship between affairs that are largely associated with the public sector (government) and those associated with the private sector (business). One purpose of this book is to examine the links between the two sectors, and to analyze the awful contradictions and gaps in the way they conduct their affairs.

The older custom of publishing timely pamphlets on current affairs has nearly vanished. It lingers only in the suspect form of hired public relations professionals who will, for appropriately commercial fees, defend or drum up some special cause. A pamphlet-length idea can be published as a relatively long article in an influential journal, but there it must share a limited readership with other articles. Another alternative is to elaborate the idea into the respectable dimensions of a full-sized book. The risk of such padding is reader boredom.

The present slim volume is offered as a sensible middle course: it is fatter than a normal pamphlet, thinner than a regular book, but still a pamphlet in spirit. It is addressed to interested and concerned readers; it deals with problems they have helped create and in any case cannot escape. The book concerns the turmoil and agonies of our times—the high-decibel rhetoric and unyielding social problems that are revealed to us with such unrelieved regularity in the daily press and on the television news.

The American university has ceased, at least for a time, to be a place insulated from the urgent cacophony of the real world. It no longer offers a sanctuary where scholars can quietly contemplate what is happening "out there," in hopes of bringing perspective, understanding, and (with luck) even guidance to practical men of affairs. The university has been thrust, perhaps irretrievably, into the real world. In fact, for a time it seemed that the university itself was where the action was.

This book is about the action "out there." The thoughts contained in it were first inflicted on a group of volunteer students at Harvard University, who debated them with me with intelligence and good grace. My thanks go to Randall W. Antik, Douglas E. Coulter, Terry R. Margerum, John A. McCullen, Eli Lipcon, Kimball Kehoe, and James D. Weinstein.

I am greatly indebted to my secretary, Rachael Daitch, for her cheerful work on so many illegible drafts of this volume—and for her consistent ability to juggle things into smooth routines under great pressure. I am also very indebted to Maria Wilhelm for her enormously helpful and intelligent assistance.

The usual apologetic reference to the indulgence and understanding of wife and children is no longer necessary. They're used to it—accustomed, with attitudes alternating between cheerfulness and resignation, to my habits. A father in his study is at least a father who is steady. Nor do I think an apology is due my regular students. It has been my undeviating intention that they should not suffer from my indulging in extracurricular academic interests. I hope the only real casualty has been my tennis.

Theodore Levitt

CONTENTS

ix

CHAPTER 1

THE AGONIZED SOCIETY

IN ITS ENTIRE HISTORY nothing has characterized American society so much as its undeviating attention to its own vaulting economic growth in the midst of intense political upheaval and abrasive discontent. In other nations political warfare and social turmoil often produce civil wars, general strikes, and long periods of paralyzing chaos, but in the United States the economic machine keeps vigorously running through thick and thin. Americans have somehow separated their general discontents and political battles from their economic affairs. They have a high tolerance for social friction—which historically has always been relieved by a new grievance's exhaustion or its success. Once the Jacksonians got the Presidency and were rid of Eastern bank control, the frontier movement petered out. Once the Populists got their Interstate Commerce Commission and the free monetization of silver, that was the end. The Mollie Mc-Guires, the Know-Nothings, the I.W.W., the CIO Organizing Committee, and McCarthyism all had short and largely undisruptive lives—undisruptive in the sense that nothing swayed the society from its main task of running the economic machine or swayed the average American from looking more to his own family and its welfare than to the supposedly bigger issues being drummed up by social activists. Only slavery produced the kind of internecine chaos that has been so common in other nations, and then only for a brief though bloody period.

All that may now be changing. America is undergoing a new and unaccustomed trauma. In the past its domestic battles centered specifically on concrete, identifiable, and technically correctable problems. Today these battles oscillate vaguely around a generalized, elusive, almost philosophic issue. The issue is not that particular problems need correction. Rather, the issue is a particular *condition* common to all our problems, one that will not be corrected by correcting the problems themselves. This condition is the way in which social power is distributed in our society and the way in which decisions are made by those who possess it.

America is undergoing a crisis of legitimacy. Suddenly numerous groups representing a wide range of discontents are vigorously challenging how the American mission of economic growth has been carried out, how decisions on social goals have been made, and how the numerous institutions and machineries that affect our lives have been managed.

The legitimacy of ancient procedures and historic institutions is being questioned: the traditions of parental authority, white supremacy, and male superiority; the freedom of teachers, bosses, and sellers to determine unilaterally, within broad limits, the nature of their relationships with those technically "beneath" them; the freedom of government agencies, the judiciary, legislative bodies, school boards, police departments, corporations, and even fraternal organizations to make their own operating and governing rules; indeed, even the freedom of a free people in a free society to do whatever they freely decide. Thus, are people free to have as many children as they wish, free to choose whom they wish freely to associate with or not associate with, free to choose whether to work or not, free to do as they wish with the natural resources and possessions they control, free to camp in public parks intended for camping, free to use without limit public roads intended for their use, free to exercise their enterprise without unreasonable restriction in an economic system that attributes its success to the fact that it is a free enterprise system?

Until recently, the negative byproducts of our material abundance were the limited concern of a select few. Now they are the energetic concern of many. Numerous new activist groups have materialized to point to our perils, demand the correction of our shortcomings, and insist on the abolition of ancient injustices. The historically inert majority has been made to see that the concerns of the few are the proper and necessary concerns of the many.

What today's social activists want is different from what they wanted in the past. In the past, they wanted specific reforms. Today they want a more responsive

3

society. Specifically, they want more responsive and benign behavior on the part of the large bureaucracies— government, corporate, judicial, professional, and educational—the big bureaucracies that make the crucial decisions that affect our lives and whose combined efforts have produced in such massive abundance precisely what America has always so undeviatingly valued.

Whether it is General Motors, the University of California, the Department of Justice, the American Medical Association, or the AFL-CIO that is being challenged and attacked, in every case the cry is for a revised ordering of national priorities and values. Quality of life, it is asserted, should have a higher priority than quantity of material goods; what quantity there is should be more equitably distributed; there should be greater public participation in determining what is equitable; and this public participation should be not just through politics but through active, interested groups and personal participation.

Each day seems to witness the creation of yet another highly agitated and determined group intent on reforming American society. These groups include the now somewhat quiescent Students for a Democratic Society, the now exhausted Black Panthers, the now fragmented ecology movement, and the still clamorous women's liberation movement. But beyond these, as we shall see, many more seek sedulously to make changes in areas where even their opponents increasingly agree things could be better.

4

Reformers and malcontents are venerable flowers on the American scene. What is new and different about today's activists is their sheer abundance, their nearly simultaneous agitation against so many long-accepted and long-honored American institutions and values, and particularly the impatient and abrasive tactics they employ with such unrestrained and self-righteous determination.

These unique characteristics of the contemporary scene—the nearly simultaneous appearance of so many anti-Establishment activists and their vigorous confrontation tactics—may create a perilous new condition in American life, even though many would agree that their discontents are often justified and their ends desirable. Their constant stream of insistent claims and abrasive tactics get us ever closer to an enveloping national pathology of brooding discontent and unrelieved suspicion, of chronic negativism and persistent fault-finding. Americans may thus come to see the nation as riddled everywhere with avarice, duplicity, injustice, indifference, and palpable evil; as so shot through with institutionalized corruption and private greed that only some sort of fundamental social upheaval can set things straight again. And the more aberrant of the activists—like the SDS and the Black Panthers in their coruscating heydays —are prepared to use any means to produce precisely such an upheaval.

Though most social activists would disagree, the main problem may now be not with the society they seek to change, but with the way they are changing society. Can we get and keep all the freedoms and material abundance we want without the accompanying traumas in economic, social, civil, and human affairs that are generated by the activists themselves?

Since a large and growing society inescapably has large and growing bureaucracies to manage its affairs, the problem is to make these bureaucracies, and indeed the whole society, properly responsive so that everybody retains some reasonable sense of his own humanity, so that important private wants and wishes are not systematically sacrificed to the implacable requirements of industrial and bureaucratic efficiency. More important, the problem is to achieve this eventuation without rancor, recrimination, or disorder.

Before it is too late, the question must be asked: How can we prevent the reformist forces which are seeking so urgently to produce a more responsive society from ruining that society in the process with their powerful new tools of social advocacy—the tools of marches, sit-ins, noise-ins, and organized accusation and vilification; their endless stream of diabolistic fault-finding in every nook and cranny of our complex world— tools whose powers are massively multiplied by the calculated exploitation of the mass media, particularly television?

In the human body, fever signals the hidden presence of something other than fever itself. "Where there's smoke, there's fire," says an ancient folk adage. Its ancientness testifies to its wisdom. The issue is not whether a particular activist group or leadership is representative of an equally aroused larger group; the issue is not whether its accusations and demands are factually correct, or justified, or legal. The real issue, as is so often the case in human and social affairs, is whether there is some other smoldering fire invisibly behind the obvious smoke, whether the fever signals a serious hidden malady.

Every person in every aspect of his life, whether he be a national leader, a business executive, a parent, a football coach, a janitor, or a child, will instinctively try to anticipate events by interpreting the weak signals sent out by their early manifestations. To wait until the signals become a wave of inevitability is to have waited too long. Thus to treat modest tremors of social unrest with seriousness—to try to see honestly what they might mean and harbor—is as natural and necessary in social as it is in private affairs.

It is therefore sensible, in this still early stage of a new form of social activism, to try to understand the reasons for its existence and for its accusatory assertions about the failure of government and business—the public and private sectors—to respond more quickly and compassionately to people's needs. Why suddenly have so many new organizations arisen to institutionalize this activism in order to tackle problems which for so many years were ignored by the other two sectors and generally tolerated by the rest of society? These new organizations—which I shall collectively call the Third Sector—demand our attention. To treat the Third Sector, its outcries and demands, its assertions and its tactics, simply as a brief though influential phase in the so-called continuing American revolution is to miss the possibility that fundamental new institutions are being created and new methods for achieving social change are being irrevocably manufactured.

CHAPTER 2

ANATOMY OF BUREAUCRACY

"CAMPAIGN G.M.; Project on Corporate Responsibility," Ralph Nader's brainchild, surfaced in the spring of 1970 and forced the world's largest manufacturing corporation to pay more attention to the social effects of its operations. Nader's tactics, and the publicity he got, were more remarkable than his objectives. The corporate community and the business press reacted to the campaign with shocked outrage, as if something terribly sinister was afoot. In the ensuing hullabaloo, people almost lost sight of Nader's relatively mild proposals. He was only trying to persuade the General Motors stockholders to *vote* for putting two "public" members on the company's 22-man board of directors, and to persuade G.M.'s management to establish an internal audit system designed to make them more aware of the social consequences of their actions and to steer their actions in more socially benign directions.

What was remarkable about this "New Left" effort, aside from the aghast corporate reaction, was its remarkably non-left orientation—its departure from ancient prescriptions that called for social revolution and the nationalization of large basic industries as the only cure for excessive social power and industrial might.

Campaign G.M. contained no abrasive slogans about public ownership or returning industry to the people. In the 1870s, after nearly three decades of preliminary rhetoric, the first serious socialist movements began in Europe. Now, in the 1970s in America, Campaign G.M. may signify the end of socialism's traditional appeal in industrial nations. In 1970 no one seemed any longer even to be using its archaic rhetoric.

The obvious fact is that the New Left disapproves of both socialism and capitalism with equal vigor; it wants one no more than it wants the other. Only the aging agitators on the other side of the generation gap still seriously believe that socialism is a solution for anything. To the young agitators, both systems are equally unresponsive. The real problem, they feel, is that society is in the iron grip of a group of involuted and bovine bureaucracies, both public and private. These bureaucracies are responsive only to one implacable internal incentive: the perpetuation of their own security and power. Created to get society's tasks done, they exist now only for themselves, no longer responsive either to their essential tasks or to society. They operate in a sealed continuum created by and for themselves. Furthermore, the old machinery for conflict resolution and social accommodation—like political participation, legislation, pressure groups, and voluntary associations—has,

in the view of the new activists, itself become bureaucratized, sluggish, and often just plain obsolete.

A generation ago in America the question of
whether the ends justified the means was at the heart
of many a long dialogue about how to solve social and
economic problems. Today many people, and especially
the active young, find this issue just as irrelevant as
Thomistic arguments about how many angels can occupy the head of a pin. To the more revolutionary agitators, it is meaningless to agonize over the question of
whether the means necessary to contain the bureaucracies are legitimate in terms of fair play or decency or
democracy. Anybody engaged in that kind of soul-
searching, they argue, has simply been seduced by the
sophistry with which bureaucracies justify their existence. Having by historically legitimate means "captured" the society, the bureaucracies—sustained by the
society's continued belief in the efficacy and necessity
of these means—now control that society. Hence, the
issue of whether the means necessary to restore society's
control over itself are themselves legitimate is beside the
point. Carried to the extreme, this view calls for a revolution by any means. Though this is stated outright by
only a radical few, it is, more quietly and euphemisti-
cally, entertained by the historically moderate many.

But each generation writes its own definition of
revolution, designs its own instruments for social change.
That they resemble or copy the past is less important
than that the present generation believes in its own dis-
tinctiveness. In the case of Campaign G.M., the activists

thought they had come up with a new solution—though in fact it wasn't new, having preceded them in other guises such as Mitbestimmung in Germany (where labor unions sit on corporate boards) two decades before. To the Old Left, Campaign G.M.'s suggestions must have seemed as flabby as they were unrealistic.

The new activists want something quite different from the old ideologues. Where the Old Left wanted "industrial democracy"—the substitution of socialist for capitalist bureaucracy—the New Left simply wants more humane organizational environments, organizations that are genuinely responsive to the broader needs of the society they so powerfully shape. The old agitators took their cues episodically from *Das Kapital*, with its pseudo-scientific documentation of the exploitative and repressive nature of capitalism as revealed in nineteenth-century Britain. The new agitators take them from the Sermon on the Mount, with its preference for moral absolutes and its belief in the superior virtue of personal revelation.

The New Left's solutions to corporate bigness and badness are solutions consisting of half natural hostility and half naive hopes—hostility toward any bureaucratic form of organization, and naïveté about the purifying possibilities of good intentions. By putting a few putative "outsiders" possessed of the right instincts on the board of directors of a $30 billion corporate colossus, and installing an inside "social audit" committee, Nader believed wrongs would be righted and more benign practices would somehow follow. Certainly this was assumed to be far better than if government tried to be the watchdog in its accustomed fumbling fashion. The New Left believes firmly in diabolism—that what is wrong is the fault of a few wrongdoers. Catch them, watch them, redirect the affairs at the top, and all will be well.

The New Left is as skeptical about public bureaucracies as it is about private bureaucracies. It firmly believes that unless they are carefully watched and badgered, bureaucracies are not likely to do any social good, even when, as in the case of various government agencies, that is their express purpose. The New Left believes that goodness is found only in incorruptibly good people. According to this view, making the corporation responsive to the general welfare calls not for government regulation or government ownership, but for planting within the corporation's complex mechanism a moral conscience in the form of incorruptible, independent watchdogs.

Nor is it just young Americans who are proposing such "solutions." Many others, too, are disenchanted with and distrustful of corporate and government bureaucracy, vigorously opposed to the existing distribution of social and economic power. Increasingly the world insists that its economic systems be productive and beneficent by measures other than a purely economic one. Similar demands are made of government. If government can behave efficiently on a large scale— for example, in war and public works—then government should also be beneficent and responsive on the individual human level. It must not blot out man while taking care of men, not create massive social machines that ignore individual human identities. Nor should government produce monstrous public edifices that sacrifice aesthetics and private habitability to institutional expediency.

The idea increasingly at large today is that the bureaucracies of private economic institutions, even when there is reasonable market competition, are not adequately responsive to the noneconomic aspirations of society. Public agencies which exist to guide and check private enterprises work poorly. They are as clumsy and unresponsive to the human condition as the bureaucracies they monitor. There is the growing feeling that the bureaucracies that have grown up to do the world's work have, by some irrepressible process, become autonomous enclaves of independent power and momentum, narrowly focusing on their own internal machinery and procedures. They see the world through the narcissistic prisms of their organizational modes. The result is a massive gap between what society wants and values and what society gets.

Unfortunately, the skepticism of the young is just about as thoughtful as the twilight ruminations of their elders. Because both are reacting emotionally to complex and intractable conditions, neither makes any serious effort at systematic analysis, and therefore neither is very helpful in charting an effective course for dealing with the causes of those conditions. But this does not mean the issues raised are any less urgent. We may be in an intermediate stage where we are simply identifying salient problems, a stage similar to the scientist's exploratory probes before solid insight and concrete explanations and solutions emerge. Ideas, with sufficient provocation and under the right circumstances, in time generate their own facilitating methodologies.

The idea that bureaucracies are rigid and unresponsive to ordinary human and social problems is nothing new. Franz Kafka, in his novel *The Trial*, long ago painted the terrible picture of a man hopelessly enmeshed in the suffocating maze of bureaucratic formalism, shuffled endlessly and impotently from one dead-end government agency to another as every succeeding functionary, pleading limited authority and anxious to protect his own flanks, passed him on to the next bloodless bureaucrat who repeated the shuffle with mechanical fidelity.

In today's world the manifestations of the problem are, in some ways, more oppressive than ever. The problem has traditionally been shrugged off as the price of progress. Material abundance requires complex economic institutions, dense cities, and elaborate and commensurately obtuse public agencies. This proposition is now under serious challenge. Must the institutions on which we depend for our benefactions be elephantine obstacles to the purposes they espouse? Must they be like massive machines wound up each morning by a master clockmaker whose only purpose is their mechanistic regularity, with no room for exceptions and no question as to antecedent or consequence?

This view of how the world is made to run drives

some of its people to the extremes of behavior in their attempts to force some measure of meliorating change: they make new kinds of noises and create new kinds of pressures in hopes of compelling new responses from machineries which, they feel, manage and administer everything except what counts. The new tactics of the new social activism are now in pathological abundance (as contrasted with only episodic occurrences in earlier times). They reflect the failure of traditional institutions and procedures to effectively hear and handle the complaints and needs of those on whom they have an impact.

But outrage and organization in support of good causes do not automatically get God's blessing. The new agitators of the Third Sector may have found and faced their enemy, but they have seldom found out what makes him tick and how to change him. Bureaucracies have certain negative characteristics, it is true, but it is useful to understand that bureaucracies serve functions which even their critics must concede can be and often are benign.

Bureaucratic formalism is not an organizational aberration. It is not an overgrown accident. It is not the planned cocoon of timorous people seeking safe anonymity. It is not the accidental consequence of men in power. It is the inescapable necessity of large-scale efficiency.

Max Weber argued before World War I that bureaucracy is the necessary consequence of organizations and that its effectiveness requires expert practitioners in its ranks.[1] A major part of Weber's argument is that experts can be effective only in the context of a formalism where whims, opinionation, and foolishness cannot intrude their contaminating influence on established norms and procedures. "Bureaucratic administration," he wrote, "means fundamentally the exercise of control on the basis of knowledge." Whenever arbitrariness or other whims of power and authority are allowed to flourish, people whose only strength is their knowledge feel their personal security threatened. That is why the staff, the professional cadre of an organization, always advocates and creates formal decision-making and operating procedures for the organization. These prevent the possibility of arbitrary decision making, which would not only make the staff obsolete but impair efficient routines. Formalism also fulfills top management's need for an orderly, predictable, and rational way of managing complexity. Thus, both line and staff functionaries will advocate, seek to preserve, and strengthen bureaucratic formalism.

Weber was quite right in suggesting that the exercise of control on the basis of knowledge is precisely the feature which makes bureaucratic administration rational. It is also the feature which makes bureaucracy go awry: ". . . technical knowledge . . . , by itself, is sufficient to ensure it a position of extraordinary power.

---

[1] Max Weber, *The Theory of Social and Economic Organization*, translated by A. M. Henderson and Talcott Parsons, edited by Talcott Parsons. New York: Oxford University Press edition, 1947.

But in addition, bureaucratic organizations, or the holders of powers who make use of them, have the tendency to increase their power still further by the knowledge growing out of experience in the service."

The consequences are socially malignant for both public and private bureaucracies. But for political democracies there is a special irony: the more democratic the electoral process, the less democratic the democratic institutions. The logic is as follows: The more democratic the society, the more frequent the elections. The more frequent the elections, the greater the turnover of elected officials and therefore the easier the access to high elective office of men who have little government and administrative experience. Hence most elected officials will have scarce knowledge of government affairs or understanding of the technical ins-and-outs of government itself. They are heavily dependent on the knowledge, advice, and work of the government's continuing professional cadre. This enhances and solidifies the nonelected cadre's power over the democratically elected occupants of political office. The elected officials circulate, getting turned in and out of power with a frequency directly proportional to the openness of the electoral system. The more rapid the circulation, the tighter the control of the cadre—and, thus, the less democratic the institutions.

From a strictly technocratic (i.e., efficiency) viewpoint, this may not be all bad. Weber felt that, despite all its shortcomings and sluggishness, bureaucratic administration is the most rational type.

For the needs of mass administration today, it is completely indispensable. The choice is only that between bureaucracy and dilettanteism in the field of administration. . . . Experience tends universally to show that the purely bureaucratic type of administrative organization . . . is, from a purely technical point of view, capable of attaining the highest degree of efficiency and is in the sense formally the most rational known means of carrying out imperative control over human beings. It is superior to any other form in precision, in stability, in the stringency of its discipline, and in its reliability. It thus makes possible a particularly high degree of calculability of results for the heads of the organization and for those acting in relation to it. It is finally superior both in intensive efficiency and in the scope of its operations, and is formally capable of application to all kinds of administrative tasks.

The bureaucratic administrative machinery we see everywhere today is not only the most efficient instrument for the operation of large-scale organizations but, in Weber's perceptive words, also performs the "crucial role in our society as the central element in any kind of large-scale administration. Only by reversion in every field—political, religious, economic, etc.—to small-scale organization would it be possible to any considerable extent to escape its influence."

But while the system of bureaucratic work is highly efficient for the execution of massive and repetitive tasks, we see everywhere the verification of Weber's words that bureaucracy entails the establishment of an exaggerated, fixed formalism. As noted earlier, the knowledge cadre encourages this formalism to ensure that its work will not be undermined by the arbitrariness of those nominally in power. But the cadre's concern with its own personal security gradually undermines its own adherence to the principles of rationalistic efficiency and professional workmanship. Thus a knowledge system that produces efficiency protects itself with formalistic procedures in order to preserve its integrity; then that very process, and its resulting institutional forms, contaminate and compromise the knowledge whose integrity was to be protected. Knowledge ceases to be the servant of efficiency and truth. Often, it also becomes the servant of those who presumably possess it. Since the higher authorities are themselves attracted to the security, predictability, and discipline imposed by these formalities, the entire spirit of large organizations will oppose any self-criticism. Bureaucracies will resist any outside criticisms or inquiries that might jeopardize their formal routines because these might jeopardize their secure existence. Insiders who make such criticisms are quickly identified as pariahs. They will be isolated, immobilized, and finally, if they persist, forced to resign. Those who cannot play the game must leave the game. Disruptive loners are viewed as poor organization men and condemned to a lonely existence on the outside.

Bureaucracies have a narrow focus, but they are, in a fashion, professional. Like all professionals, bureaucracy's professionals have a constant preoccupation with the cultivation and preservation of professional repute.

This requires careful (though generally unconscious) protection against outside criticism; the establishment and enforcement of appropriate standards of public decorum for its members; the discouragement of unseemly self-criticism, even in private; and a cultivated display of public receptiveness combined with hardened private resistance to any changes in the profession's inherited practices and dogmas.

Taken all together, this produces organizational inefficiency—but also a very special kind of bureaucratic efficiency. The large, professionally run bureaucratic organization gets its work done, but in the process develops a kind of rote impersonality guaranteed to draw criticisms of insensitivity and unresponsiveness—insensitivity to the larger public's needs and problems, and unresponsiveness to demands that it change its dealings with individuals on the inside or the whole society on the outside. It is not that the organization is composed of bad men, but rather of mechanical men. All this was fully foreseen by Weber: the organization, he said, would be characterized by the "dominance of a spirit of formalistic impersonality, 'Sine ira et studio,' without hatred or passion, and hence without affection or enthusiasm."

That is precisely what much of the discontent of our times is about—reaction against the seemingly cold, passionless, and unresponsive character of our public and private institutions, and especially their seeming indifference to criticisms about their negative human and social consequences. To many who must deal with them, it appears that our institutions operate in a sealed continuum and can only be shaken out of their respectable impassiveness by confrontation and force. That is why confrontation tactics are such popular tools of the new social activists. They have despaired of the traditional tools of persuasion and ordinary political pressure. As they see it, either the bureaucracies have learned ways of not responding to tactics that worked in simpler times, or they are simply deaf.

It has long been accepted that bureaucratic organizations are the inevitable consequence of complex industrial societies, and that complex industrial societies are the inevitable consequence of the drive for economic abundance. If these premises are accepted, a less bureaucratized world is not in the cards. Everywhere people want abundance. Though in the more abundant societies they talk nostalgically of simpler times, in practice they go for all available modern goods and services. People may be substituting bicycles for cars, vegetables for meat, and sneakers for dress shoes, but such changes in tastes do not alter the need for large-scale organization. As long as society values and wants the things which only large combinations of technology can deliver economically, there will be large economic enterprises governed by the principles of rational bureaucracy; and there will have to be similar and to some extent offsetting government bureaucracies.

This is the question, then: How can a society which generally approves of the material abundance produced by modern industrial bureaucracies, and of the public benefits emanating from government bureaucracies, protect itself against their adverse effects? How can it penetrate the seeming pride and arrogance of bureaucracies, their unresponsiveness to private individuals, their resistance to public wants that do not fit into their own inflexible routines or fixed procedures? The issue is not that bureaucracy is superfluous; the issue is how the dominant bureaucracies of our times can be made more compassionate and responsible while performing on a mass scale the jobs that, it is generally agreed, must continue to be done in somewhat the same fashion they are being done today.

This does not mean that all bureaucracies are automatically efficient, or that they are all smugly unconcerned with social problems. Those on the inside seldom admit in public their own doubts about how well their institution is working. But judging from the evidence in recent years, they obviously have a lot of doubts.

In the world in general, and especially in America, there is a rising tendency for larger business firms to create their own internal counterforces and watchdogs against their own possible inadequacies. Special study groups and task forces have sprung up in the large corporations to audit the effectiveness of many of their activities, examine the wisdom of many of their policies, and even inquire into the human and social consequences of what they do. Management consultants are in abundance, thriving on fees from companies seeking an independent outside look. Similarly, large organizations are creating venture teams and new business development departments which they hope will bring systematically into their bureaucratic orbits the entrepreneurial equivalent of what smaller and more agile companies do more commonly with no special effort. And in government we have seen the periodic creation of such high-level study groups as the Hoover Commission after World War II and the Ash Advisory Council on Executive Organization. In both big business and big government, the aim is to achieve more effectiveness than existing arrangements seem capable of yielding.

In short, bureaucracies are trying to better themselves. When questioned, their managements will say that they do not necessarily think something is wrong; it is just that they believe they can do better. And yet many members of bureaucracies *do* believe something is wrong. In an ever widening circle, doubt spreads—even within outwardly self-assured organizations—as to whether the way things work is really as inexorable as they have always believed. There is awkward doubting about the immutability of the laws of competition, the iron laws of economics, and the textbook rules of the organizational process. Should their mechanistic verdicts be so complacently accepted as inevitable? Or might not some things be beneficially changed according to man's wishes, even at some sacrifice of what has always been called economic progress or efficiency?

These questions are increasingly asked, but they also produce a lot of resistance, even among the askers. Part of the resistance stems from fear for the pristine purity of the free enterprise system. But more important, the resistance indicates a deeper anxiety—the fear of introducing irrationality and caprice into the management of organizations. It is this possibility that poses the greatest of all threats to those now securely on the inside. Reform is interpreted not so much as loss of power or authority, but as loss of control—the obsolescence of hard-learned competences. After all these years of learning how to function in the system, what will happen if the rules get changed? That is the main and haunting reason why bureaucratic organizations have great difficulty reforming themselves from the inside.

One of Weber's special insights about bureaucracies is their tendency to construct insulating devices for the security of their functionaries. Bureaucracies are manned by cadres of experts and technicians who, operating in organizations characterized by extreme division of labor, specialize in the knowledge of their specialties. They know all the theories, use all the data, and have all the accompanying skills with which to practice their special arts. But men who work largely with their minds, who do not directly participate in the production of a tangible product or directly manage other people who produce one, occupy fragile positions in an organization. They are exceedingly vulnerable to suggestions of their expendability. For the highly trained professional, the more tangible the output of the organization in which he works—say, producing weapons or dog food or even consulting reports—the more fragile is his position in that organization. He doesn't visibly create *things*.

Under the circumstances, blind instinct for survival, if nothing else, would explain the self-protecting actions and sophistries of bureaucrats. Of course they do exactly what would be expected: In order to preserve their organizational power, and thereby protect their jobs, they constantly assert the utility of their knowledge and the arts they practice. In time, they build elaborate zones of insulation to shield them against the possibility of anybody effectively questioning their usefulness— which could lead to the worse possibility of their being fired.

Thus the specialized expert in the formal bureaucratic organization is always adept at explaining how complex the problem at hand really is and how grave are the risks of proceeding without studying it further and at considerable depth. He also excels in explaining that certain things simply cannot be done and other things simply must be done. He seriously believes what he advises, and often he is indisputably right. But it must be remembered that this is one of the major ways he has of expanding, or at least preserving, his power and his job. Not that other people in other circumstances don't also care about their job tenure. But people who are directly employed in producing tangible outputs have less need and opportunity to employ these tactics. Everybody can see that they do what is called a productive day's work.

This helps explain why government bureaucracies are so much more rigid and less responsive than private bureaucracies. Because they produce fewer tangible outputs, their staffs are more defensive. It also explains why the Pentagon, which produces more palpable social products than other government bureaucracies, has such disproportionate power within the government.

The fairly narrow task of the bureaucratic specialist reinforces indifference to its consequences. Each bureaucrat has his own function, which he performs more according to that function's demands than out of concern for its particular consequences. He does not raise the broader question of what it is all for, or about possible harmful results. The chemical engineer focuses on making a better and cheaper plastic bottle, without a thought to congestion in the municipal incinerator. The hair-cream advertising executive focuses on how best to ensnare a customer, without speculating whether the customer might be better off using the money for his intellectual rather than his cosmetic improvement. The organizer of a school-bond syndicate does not ask what the school will teach. The federal highway engineer does not ask about other uses for highway funds. Nor does the lathe operator in the automobile factory ask why we make new models every year or the Department of Labor statistician whether it is really worth making yet another study of wage differentials in the needle trades. His job is to know all there is to know about needle trades wage differentials. For him, the fact that he has been assigned the job is sufficient. The machinery operates without asking why, precisely because each functionary performs so narrow a task and his family needs are so compelling that it is pointless to ask.

At the opposite extreme from the bureaucrat who performs pointless tasks is the bureaucrat who makes policy in the process of doing his prescribed work. When specialists in the U.S. Department of Housing and Urban Development lay down specifications for a federal housing project—establishing a particular ratio of occupied to open land, a particular number of rooms for particular-sized families, and various facilities for recreation, parking, laundry, and ventilation—they are in effect setting policies regarding minimum life styles in America. Yet these policies are being laid down by functionaries who have no charter from the electorate to make policy. Clark Clifford, former Secretary of Defense, summarized the Washington facts succinctly: "The overwhelming majority of decisions is made at the staff level." As we have seen, the more frequent the elections, the less frequently elected officials control the government's work. The more powerful its bureaucracy, the less democratic the democracy.

Nor are private bureaucracies entirely exempt from these conditions. In business the output is generally more tangible and the effects of competition—if it exists with some intensity and regularity—are more chastening. This mitigates against the uneven reign of the entrenched bureaucratic cadre, but the results are not always so different. Competition is seldom all that compelling. The desire for personal power and security is much the same as in government. And—in big business, at any rate—the problems require just as much staff expertise. The *culture* of private bureaucracies is therefore basically the same as that of public bureaucracies, different though the two may be in the tunes to which they march.

They also have basically the same source of funds. Public bureaucracies are tax-financed, which to some extent puts them at the mercy of the public's ability and willingness to pay taxes. Similarly, the public's ability and willingness to buy goods and services determines what funds a private bureaucracy will have. But there is a difference, at least in most capitalist societies: the public generally has a choice of buying from several private bureaucracies, but it has little choice of which public bureaucracy to "buy" from. In this respect, the two types of bureaucracies operate in quite different contexts. Business knows that the public's choice depends, in part, on the efficiency with which business operates and the reflection of that efficiency in the price of its products. Business must be responsive to the public (the market) because it is constantly tested by the buyers: Are the products the right ones, designed right, packaged right, available in a sufficient variety of styles and sizes, available in easily accessible places, priced right?

All this imposes a discipline on most private bureaucracies that is not present in public bureaucracies. The absence of this discipline accounts for the greater lethargy of public bureaucracies, their relative sluggishness, and their greater concern with building barriers against interference from both the outside and the inside. The differing ways business and government organizations are financed, and the differing degrees of continuing external pressures to which they are subjected, explain why there is a lot more management in business than in government bureaucracies. Government bureaucracies are generally characterized by administration; business bureaucracies by management.

The most important distinction between administration and management is that the former performs custodial tasks, the latter sets priorities. Administration deals largely with routines; management, with choices. While every organization has some system of priorities, whether explicit or not, organizations exposed to continuing marketplace pressures are almost automatically pressured into having and periodically reexamining and rearranging their priorities. Those that do not tend finally to go out of business. Public organizations at best reexamine their priorities at election time. But because elections come in infrequent though predictable cycles, and because elected officials are often new or temporary to the task, the bureaucratic cadre of government is generally capable of manipulating any reexamination to its own professional and self-protective ends—and often it does just that. Thus the elected leaders to some extent become the captives of the administrative staffs that nominally exist to carry out their wills. As President Kennedy remarked when urged to a new course of action by a White House assistant, "I agree with you, but will the government?"

Once their priorities are established, private and public bureaucracies operate about the same. Both are characterized by the efficient administration of generally repetitive and specialized tasks. Because they are alike in this highly important way, it might be assumed that one of them, acting as surveillant and watchdog of the other, would be well suited to understanding and investigating the other. But it is precisely because they are basically so alike that one is an unreliable overseer of the other: bureaucratic professionals will not generally question or attack each other's basic security.

For example, the Federal Power Commission's staff has never suggested that any private electric company has done a poor job and therefore should be nationalized, or that small, inefficient private companies should be amalgamated. Although amalgamations would eliminate redundant bureaucracies, this would violate one of the most sacred bureaucratic tenets, namely, that all bureaucies are indispensable. Professional ethics preclude the suggestion of the obsolescence of one by another. When one bureaucracy oversees another, the best that can be expected is that the regulator will keep the regulated sensibly and securely protected from offending outsiders and even from overzealous infiltrators in their own ranks. One major exception to this rule is when the head of a given government bureaucracy has political ambitions (say, a district attorney) which can be advanced by his investigating and publicly attacking private bureaucracies. Another exception is when things have gone so badly for so long in a regulated company that the regulator finally overcomes its natural tendencies and recommends consolidation—as in the case of the nation's ailing railroads.

Thus the nominally contending public and private

bureaucracies have a natural desire to maintain a benign equilibrium between them. This equilibrium is, however, in continuing jeopardy. Young, inexperienced, or insufficiently acculturated new members of bureaucracies constantly threaten by overzealousness to disrupt the unspoken, mutually accommodating arrangements that set operative limits on mutual criticism and snooping, arrangements that get deeply entrenched over many years. In government affairs we see the repeated, by now almost predictable, spectacle of youthful functionaries being precipitously dismissed or resigning in a splashy huff, charging that they were prevented by the government itself from rigorously enforcing government laws and regulations.

Though public regulatory agencies operate within these limits, adhering to implicit standards of "fair play" and limited criticism of the private bureaucracies they supposedly regulate, this does not mean that these agencies are entirely ineffective. They are effective within the established limits, and—ironically—they are effective in resisting when the limits themselves are tested by either side for openings or weaknesses. If some rude, inexperienced, or clumsy party fails to maintain acceptable decorum during such tests, or if the tests are abrasive or embarrassing for either side, the reaction is often commensurately tough and embarrassing for the transgressor.

Everything points irresistibly to the conclusion that under ordinary circumstances government bureaucracies are not much to be relied upon for making business bureaucracies more responsive and responsible. Nor, as already noted, are more frequent and democratic elections likely to improve things.

Certainly the New Left has criticized government for its failure to regulate business and for its own internal sluggishness. But the vast majority of its criticisms have been directed at business. When one considers again the source of business' funds, it becomes apparent that business is often criticized by some for doing what is wanted by others.

Business has always, in a sense, been responsive to public needs because it depends on its ability to attract and hold customers at a profit. The public "votes" for or against a business firm in the iron crucible of a relatively impartial marketplace. But it is a self-centered vote, seldom as totally manipulated by the advertiser as some who speak more from belief than from fact would have us believe. In 1955, the very year that Senator Estes Kefauver's investigation of General Motors dealer practices created such a prolonged anti-G.M. front-page furor, Chevrolet had its biggest sales in history. The public seldom votes its political views or aspirations for the community with its household budget. Few men with limited cash will take their business to the higher-priced seller whose social policies they prefer. Money, after all, is money. Its most compelling characteristics are scarcity and difficulty of acquisition. This imposes a discipline on its private use that lofty social consciousness seldom sways.

Business, moreover, has many different and often conflicting constituencies. A factory making high-quality, low-cost writing paper in upstate New York may thereby produce for itself great profits and for the public in New York City great satisfaction, but a hundred miles up the Hudson River it may produce great dissatisfaction in towns suffering from the factory's smelly effluent. Stopping the effluence would, at least in the short run, raise prices and thereby reduce both the firm's competitiveness and New York City's satisfaction. To the factory, it scarcely matters whether the declining consumer satisfaction due to higher paper costs is balanced by increasing upstate satisfaction due to lesser pollution. For it, pollution is a negative externality not conveniently considered in its own cost-benefit calculations. Only the whole society acting collectively can make and benefit from such calculations.

But even if society could make accurate cost-benefit calculations, there is no reason why it should be all that interested in pure efficiency. Society is not business, and it is interested in lots more things than business. Business is interested in efficiency—its own efficiency. Society is interested in fairness—everybody's fairness. And fairness, which includes amenities and life styles as well as measurable quantities like wages, has little to do with cost-benefit calculations. That is why large organizations have been so consistently tardy in responding to changed social and political sentiments. Even though large business firms hire full-time specialists and costly consultants to help them "anticipate impacts" and "do their social duty," when profits are at stake their major thrust is exactly what one would expect. When the bottom simultaneously fell out of the automobile market and the stock market in the spring of 1970, the Chrysler Corporation silently dropped its hard-core-unemployed training program in the very week that its president agreed to head the National Alliance of Businessmen, whose major purpose was to promote the training of the hard-core unemployed by American firms. The larger companies may have more public relations muscle to proclaim their good deeds, but in the end the local butcher or grocer may quietly do lots more.

Some American businesses realize that they cannot see very well by themselves where society is headed or fathom its changing wants and values. This realization has now reached marketable proportions, as evidenced by the recent launching of at least two private social forecasting services whose regular reports are available to business at prices commensurate with their pretensions: $25,000 a year for one of them. Some corporations, newly aware of their limitations in these areas and their resulting vulnerability to criticism, actually subscribe to both services. What the subscribing corporations will or can do with these services remains to be seen. Simply to *have* another's informed opinion about society's current or prospective needs does not guarantee any ability or willingness to do anything about them, especially if what needs doing lies outside the historic competence or easy inclination of the corporation. Even government, whose business presumably is to do something about these things, debates endlessly about whether to do anything, and if so what, and if what, with how much commitment and funds. This suggests that corporations, which do *not* have the job of doing anything about them, will probably do very little unless strongly urged by new social pressure. Nor will they eagerly urge the government to respond. Indeed, if past experience is any indication of what the future holds, the one assurance we have is that corporations will vigorously oppose any government efforts to make them respond to the very needs uncovered by the forecasting services to which they subscribe. This follows logically from their function: business functions best when the environment in which it operates changes least. Business, which already has to contend with changes created by the ordinary forces at work in the environment, sees governmental attempts to create even more changes—by means of legislation, decree, or reinterpretation of existing laws—as an intolerable compounding of already difficult conditions. Ideologically, nothing is better suited to the conservative business temperament than the 1776 revolutionary slogan, "That government which governs least governs best." When pressured to change quickly or drastically in the interest of what others assert is the public good, business responds slowly—and most commonly only as a last resort.

The most compelling illusion of bureaucracy is the idea that the problem of bureaucratic unresponsiveness can be solved by creating more bureaucracies. When confronted with problems that lie either within or outside of its specialized orbit, a bureaucracy is always tempted to turn to institutionalized surveillance and control in the hope that new bureaucracies will come up with new ideas and new actions.

Nor does self-policing achieve much responsiveness, within either private or public bureaucracies. Watchdog committees, intercessionists, and ombudsmen have repeatedly proved their ineffectualness—their appointment always announced with glowing, self-righteous press releases, but their subsequent impotence never confessed and their final euthanasia never celebrated. By their very nature, bureaucratic organizations cannot undo or cleanse their own bureaucratic compulsions—or those of others. Individuals who are charged with the self-correction or transformation of a bureaucracy find that any such effort violates the very conditions of the bureaucracy. In the end, it is the individuals, not the bureaucracies, that get transformed. Hear the confession of one who tried in P. H. Newby's novel, *A Guest and His Going* [2]: "From that moment he had been part of the organization—adapting himself, gaining something there but conceding more here, fitting in, deferring, adjusting, trimming. After years of administration he couldn't be really rude to people any more, even to Brush. He tried but it was never really effective."

There is an even more important reason why self-policing is not likely to work: What people object to is

[2] New York: Alfred A. Knopf, 1960.

not what the large bureaucracies purposely do, but rather what happens as the accidental consequence of what they are supposed to do. They are supposed to be efficient in the exercise of their acknowledged purposes. Yet it is precisely their workmanlike pursuit of these purposes that produces, from another viewpoint, certain negative consequences. The efficient assembly line may produce faceless and disparaged workers. The effective union bargaining session with a large employer requires lawyers and economists from union headquarters negotiating on big national issues that minimize the urgency of perhaps more immediately pressing though minor local issues. The clear and precise written rules that are needed to govern the activities of a corporate subsidiary or a government agency cannot anticipate all future exceptions, anomalies, or even routines, and so to achieve their primary duties they must frequently ignore, forget, or postpone the uncommon. Bureaucratic unresponsiveness is often a necessary and not altogether accidental byproduct of bureaucratic efficiency.

Bureaucratic unresponsiveness to human and social conditions is created by the bureaucracies' technocratic attention to their main tasks in a world that changes faster than its organizational practices either can or want to change. Conventional bureaucracies by definition cannot tolerate unconventional methods in their midst. Every new American President since 1933 has, upon his inauguration, put eager young men in positions of high authority. Each time, some of these youthful zealots got quickly fired for doing too well their jobs of "assuring the public welfare." Unaccustomed to the ways of large organizations, they found themselves outside when they failed to work in the accustomed manner inside. If this so regularly happens in the highly visible fishbowls of Washington, D.C., it is certain that inside the protected walls of private firms equally zealous advocates who rock the boat will get fired even faster, or at least get quickly reassigned to Lower Slobovia.

In recent years, private industry has been particularly attracted to the possibility of improving its own affairs and effectiveness by the use of specialized task forces, venture teams, and study groups. The results have been notably unimpressive.

Corporate task forces charged with providing self-criticism and self-renewal have exhibited a chronic inability to call a spade a spade. Considering that the task force members were trained in the methods and norms of the very bureaucratic enterprises they were asked to judge, one should not be surprised at the outcome. The best of intentions are no match for the quietly effective acculturation which qualified them for appointment to the task force in the first place. There will be systematic avoidance of hard criticism and no admission of basic faults. By its composition, the task force is predisposed to produce soft results. Nobody must get hurt.

When the conditioning is as thorough as it is in most large organizations, effective internal self-analysis is the rarest of occurrences, especially on matters that lie outside the organization's routines and traditional competence.

As for venture teams, as long as they must depend on the existing corporate management for final approval of their entrepreneurial projects, they are subject to precisely the conventional corporate standards and routines they were designed to escape. Men who have risen to the managerial top of complex organizations by a combination of energy, intelligence, character, and good bureaucratic performance are not likely suddenly to make decisions on the basis of methods or standards other than those to which they owe their eminence. The circle is therefore closed against any real possibility that audacity or entrepreneurship will escape the rigid managerial routine. Neither venture teams nor study teams, being creatures of the managerial cultures that created them, will in practice become the independent sources of criticism and energy that they were intended to become. They end up being the reinforcing arms of the bureaucracy that created them.

As we have seen, large organizations, being large, must operate according to a fairly rigid and predictable routine. That is the only way to achieve control and realize the economies of scale (whether in manufacturing, distribution, administration, or finance) that are the purpose of largeness. Just as a worker assigned the specific task of, say, attaching a rear-view mirror on each passing automobile on an assembly line cannot be allowed the initiative of attaching two mirrors or a mirror of his own design, so random entrepreneurship cannot be permitted in the administration or management of a large enterprise. Predictable routine is the standard requirement, and that becomes the corporate culture.

Of the large organizations that have tried internal study and venture teams, I know of few that can honestly claim any real success. Some exceptions have been organizations undergoing deep fiscal crisis, like the Ford Motor Company after World War II. Only when an organization begins to crumble do the cracks and fissures get deep enough for radical new ideas and new men to enter and gain a foothold. Other exceptions are companies that have been forced into significantly different patterns by powerful outsiders, generally from the financial community.

In the case of the American government, the inevitable suggestion for solving the problems of apathy, inefficiency, obsolescence, and other bureaucratic vices has been to substitute "sound" management for "routine" administration. That was the recommendation of the Hoover Commission after World War II and later of the Ash Advisory Council. The Ash Council's recommendations led to the establishment of the Office of Management and Budget. The council later proposed a complex merging of federal agencies under a more centralized arrangement, proclaiming that this would make them easier to manage and coordinate. Significantly, the Ash Council proposals involved no reduction or real structural alteration of existing bureaucracies. They merely added new coordinating groups or consolidated existing administrations. In the end there was no change, only rearrangement and addition.

The difficulty of changing bureaucracies is not entirely due to the self-protective insulations that the bureaucratic culture has built for itself. Another reason is simply that we need them. Existing tasks must somehow continue to be performed. And in a large, complex society, their performance depends precisely on the kind of mechanized and passionless routine that already exists. Sometimes it is simply proposed that bureaucracies be reduced in size. But it is only at the rhetorical level that reduction seems possible. Many of President Nixon's much-heralded 1973 reductions and eliminations of government programs seem already on their way to reinstatement.

Thus bureaucracies do create formal, internal mechanisms for organizational self-analysis and self-renewal, and government does create continually bigger and better-financed government agencies to regulate and audit private industry. But these actions are only the ritualistic process by which policy-making organizational potentates substitute form for action, fooling themselves that having created the machinery to produce results they have assured the attainment of results. The ironic consequences of this process were never more powerfully demonstrated than in General Motors' response in 1970 to the Campaign G.M. demand for "public" board members and a watchdog committee to assure that the corporation attacked the automobile pollution problem more vigorously. After much resistance, General Motors appointed a five-man watchdog committee —all board members from "outside" G.M. itself, to be sure, but one member was the president of a chemical company that itself had big pollution problems, and another member was a bank president whose family controlled 27 percent of a major oil producing and refining company and a half-dozen other corporations that were the object of considerable antipollution agitation. In an ultimate example of inbred bureaucratic blindness at work, the General Motors board chairman expressed wounded surprise when his choices were instantly criticized from many quarters.

The obvious conclusion to all this is that today's bureaucracies, though unwieldy and unresponsive in many respects, are necessary and inescapable, unless of course we are prepared to turn the clock back to the reduced living standards that a fragmented and simpler preindustrial system entails. Since only a utopian fringe of society is willing to do that, the problem is how to preserve the material and organizational benefits of large organizations while simultaneously making them more compassionate regarding the human and social consequences of their massive mechanical routines.

People most deeply involved in the actual machinery of business and government bureaucracies know that neither their elimination, fragmentation, closer surveillance, nor replacement with various revolutionary alternatives will solve the problem of bureaucratic unresponsiveness and sluggishness. Nor can it be solved by somehow shifting the emphasis of bureaucracies from mechanistic efficiency to human responsiveness. That would only create confusion and indecisiveness, a failure to do anything well because of uncertain and shifting standards. Nobody would know for sure which master to serve—the demands of the market one day, of the polity the next, of a pushy pressure group the next, or of some private dream the next. The result would be inefficiency, disorder, perhaps even chaos, especially in the performance of tasks that require formalism and routine.

The problem is how to get large bureaucracies to continue to do their bureaucratic jobs with their accustomed narrow efficiency while also making them quickly aware of and effectively responsive to the social and human consequences of their actions.

Fortunately, the answer lies precisely in the nature of the bureaucratic organization itself. The sudden disruption of its routine is its greatest vulnerability. This is the secret discovered by Nader and others of the Third Sector.

I have not meant to imply in this chapter that large organizations are not responsive in some fashion to public needs and clamor. Indeed, in recent years there has been enormous responsiveness on many matters—witness civil rights, minority employment, Medicare, reconsideration of massive slum clearance and urban highway projects, student participation in academic decision making, electoral reform, consumer protection, environmental melioration, maternity leaves, job enrichment programs, and so forth. However, all evidence points to the conclusion that the recent responsiveness of our complex private and public organizations, including our legislatures, has been brought about largely by the insistent confrontation tactics of organizations from the Third Sector. Few of the major meliorating responses of the last decade can be attributed to the conventional machinery of social protest or to the conventional machinery of legislative and administrative processes. The initiative and the continuing pressure came from the Third Sector, and it was publicity, not violence, that was responsible for most of its successes. Nothing more reliably sends a corporate chief executive scurrying quickly back from vacation than a damaging front-page accusation against his company. Nothing more reliably assures a fast and well-phrased public relations denial.

Significantly, however, the immediate purpose of these denials (and other such actions) relates more to the corporate bureaucracy's vested concern with itself than to the public's need for action. This is evident from the fact that the denials are largely aimed at the corporations' own employees. The best indication of that is that such denials, together with a special, intimate covering letter from the chief executive, are, in the best-run bureaucracies, quickly circulated to every member of the organizational cadre. Presidential letters to employees are almost exclusively limited to such crisis situations, and seldom are used to announce or discuss general corporate matters or policies. This is the ultimate silent testament to what the organization is really concerned about in these matters: not talking about what the organization does and why (because it is unquestioningly assumed that the organization should be doing what it does) but talking back at critics who endanger the routine and undermine morale.

Still, there is evidence that chief executives do more than merely talk back. With sufficient provocation from the right sources they actually do something about the problems or failures for which they are under outside attack. Perhaps they do less than some might hope, but things happen. The trick for the chief executive is to make them happen in a routine rather than a hasty and short-sighted fashion. Thus when the Coca-Cola Company was publicly attacked in the summer of 1970 for fostering unseemly living conditions of the migrant workers at its orange groves, the company did not rush out quickly merely to put up, say, neat new, placating mobile homes. Instead, Paul Austin, Coca-Cola's chief executive, set into motion a far-ranging program to build new housing, raise wages, and include the citrus pickers in many of the nonwage benefits enjoyed by permanent Coca-Cola employees. The bureaucracy, once moved to take action, took it in smooth, effective, and professional style. Through a complete and carefully detailed program of amelioration, things were changed but not upset.

Bureaucracy is very competent at protecting itself against threats to its stability. First, it is exceedingly sensitive to conditions that it believes create stress. Second, when it wants to it can respond very effectively to such conditions. From the public viewpoint, the problem is that so few conditions create the kind of palpable stresses to which bureaucracy responds constructively.

Apparently criticism must be loud and visible, even abrasive; it must be seemingly well documented; and above all, it must be totally unexpected. To routinize criticism and limit it to predictable sources is to neutralize criticism. It loses its novelty, its authority, its bite.

There are, in fact, many well-intentioned sources of criticism that have lost their bite because of their predictability, their unwillingness to rock the boat, and their limited power. These will be discussed in the following chapter.

CHAPTER 3

THE THIRD SECTOR

PERSUASION AND PULL

ALTHOUGH business and government may not be adequately responsive in the sense we have been talking about—whether on purpose, from ignorance, or by bureaucratic default—this does not mean that society as a whole is unresponsive. Indeed, the opposite is generally true. It is useful to look at the rest of society to see what happens when its more formally organized sectors are deaf or insular or preoccupied.

The conventional taxonomy divides society into two sectors—private and public. Private is business. Public is presumed to be all else. But "all else" is too broad; it covers so much that it means nothing. In terms of how society's work gets done, the most relevant component of "all else" is government. Its activities, influence, and power are so salient, even in the least governmentalized of nations, that it qualifies at least as well as business as a special sector unto itself. In common parlance, "the public sector" refers to those things that government does, can do, or ought to do. But that leaves an enormous residuum, which itself is divisible in many ways.

I have called this residuum the Third Sector. It is composed of a bewildering variety of organizations and institutions with differing degrees of visibility, power, and activeness. Although they vary in scope and specific purposes, their general purposes are broadly similar—to do things business and government are either not doing, not doing well, or not doing often enough. The existence of a Third Sector reflects the failure (sometimes the deliberate reluctance or refusal) of the business and government sectors of society to deal with many of the human, economic, and social problems that they were often created or widely assumed somehow to solve, or that have never been assumed to be the province of any specified sector. The existence of the Third Sector often reflects the failure of the other sectors to be adequately concerned with the negative, though generally unintended, consequences of their own actions.

There has always been a Third Sector. In the past, it operated quietly in the interstices between business and government, largely ignored by social commentators. It included the church, fraternal organizations, labor unions, and a vast assortment of task-oriented voluntary groups such as symphony associations, the Salvation Army, associations for the blind and crippled, neighborhood associations, and the Audubon Society.

Third Sector organizations have purposes, just like businesses and governments. Often they operate cheek by jowl with business and government. Their objectives and social consequences may be the same as or related to those of business and government. But the sectors are clearly different. And the clearest of the differences is not in their activities or goals, but rather in the social tools they employ.

That man is a tool-using animal is a truth so obvious that we avoid cliche by avoiding the observation. Man's use of tools extends far beyond the alleviation of physical work or the facilitation of mechanical results. There is also social work. Business gets its work done through the tool of exchange, and effective exchange requires the rational calculation of competitive economics. Although individual businesses differ greatly, varying in size, industry characteristics, operating styles, and the extent to which they are subjected to various social controls, businesses everywhere are remarkably homogeneous in their basic forms and disciplines. Business' ultimate organizing principle is the commercial marketplace, even in socialist societies. If those who make up the market, whether scattered private consumers or organized public commissars, are not satisfied with what comes to market and at what price, the producer is in trouble.

Thus, exchange (or commerce) is common to the economic processes of all societies. Furthermore, even in the most utopian of systems, business is always carried on through some agreed medium of exchange—which may be currency, beads, work chits, or an implicit community consensus about the values inherent in a barter. Whether the institutions involved are privately or publicly owned, their function is the efficient production and delivery of the goods and services that society requires. In capitalist nations this process is largely carried on by business organizations—by what we call the private sector.

The tools of government are clearly different. Government's distinctive tool is law—the power of compulsion, especially in domestic affairs. While government lays down many policies that do not explicitly have the force of law, they always have law's implicit sanction. Even despots impelled by little more than lust for personal power seek to legitimize their arbitrary actions, often by baptizing them with the false respectability of contrived legislation or popular vote. The Soviet Congress of the Communist Party is asked to stamp its ritual approval on decisions already made. General Franco imposes compulsory participation in periodic elections in order to provide total ratification of his dictatorial deeds. Legitimacy, real or contrived, is the quest of all governments. Law is the formal codification of legitimacy; it is the seminal tool of government.

Of course, law is not government's only tool. Every government, socialist or capitalist, offers a wide panoply of inducements and incentives to get what it wants: tax abatements to encourage capital investment and exports, vacation villas on the Caspian Sea, munificent cash gifts for not growing cotton.

As we have seen, in spite of all the energy that business and government expend on a wide range of social and economic activities, many of society's needs are not met by their ever expanding orbits. There are needs that have not been translated into markets. There are problems that have not been attacked or solved by laws. Neither do these needs and problems get entirely taken care of by such ancient institutions as the family. So new institutions, neither "private" nor "public" in the usual sense, continually emerge to try their hand. These are the Third Sector. It too has its distinctive technology, or tools. The central functional tool of the Third Sector has historically been voluntarism. It has depended largely on voluntary donations of time and money, and on quiet persuasion, to get results. Historically its province has been the untackled and unfinished work of business and government, and often of the unintended problems created by their existence.

Industrial labor unions are an obvious example. Specialized business organizations dedicated single-mindedly to relatively narrow tasks generally produce new problems external to the tasks being performed. When the quest for industrial efficiency and profits finally went too far and the times were right, industrial unions arose in an attempt to institutionalize concern for the workers in industry.

Neither unions nor charitable organizations are as obviously needed in society as government (which makes and keeps the rules) or as economic organizations (which make and distribute our food, shelter, and conveniences). Thus the voluntary nature of Third Sector institutions can be explained by the fact that their social purposes are less obviously critical. For most people, participation in Third Sector organizations is not required by law or motivated by the need for income, though it may be motivated by the wish to protect income. The cement that binds Third Sector organizations together is therefore different from the other sectors. Their appeal is to voluntarism, whereas the other sectors depend on law and commercial pressure.

Economic institutions rely on the strategic and efficient deployment of capital to get their way. Government institutions rely on the strategic and efficient deployment of law to get theirs. Third Sector institutions have traditionally relied on persuasion, augmented at times by the power of numbers. While no adult in need of food and shelter can for long escape participation in some economic institution, and none can ever escape the rule of law (or its close relative, the force of custom), nobody is ever forced to the same degree to join any Third Sector institution or be subjected to its influences.

Not that voluntarism—even idealism—is entirely lacking in the private and public sectors. There may be no escape from the necessity of government and economics, but neither is there any necessity that everything they touch be done solely by calculating rationalists employing only the space-age tools of their trades. The real difference between participating as a functionary in the private or public sector on the one hand, and in the Third Sector on the other, is primarily a difference in rewards. Participants in the first two sectors generally seek financial compensation first; personal satisfaction, power, or prestige secondarily (except perhaps in the higher echelons of government, where prestige and power may be primary); and only then to be of some general service to society. The rewards sought by Third Sector participants are almost wholly to serve some social or human purpose. They generally earn their daily bread in other ways. Though the more formal and venerable Third Sector institutions have small full-time staffs to carry on at the administrative core, numerous volunteers continue to work at the operating periphery. Even though some of its members earn other rewards, the Third Sector's preeminent characteristic is still voluntarism.

Because Third Sector membership is uniquely voluntary, its organizations lack the automatic authority and power of the other two. Institutions that are absolutely necessary from day to day are almost automatically vested with the powers needed to keep them functioning. Voluntary institutions are vested only with the powers they assume and assert. Their power depends first on their capacity to enlist volunteer support and then on the amount of money they are able to acquire for their purposes. Sometimes they are financed by voluntary contributions from the public, campaigns for which may be organized by resolutely profit-making firms that specialize in the crisp, professional procurement of funds. Sometimes they are financed by tax-free endowments or membership fees. And there are other arrangements. Whatever the case, the money-making efforts are largely made possible by the voluntary contribution of their supporters' time and energy. These supporters have usually used simple persuasion to get money to finance their causes.

The National Urban League is as good an example as any of how persuasion and money have been used in tandem. Though the League operates quite differently these days, in the past the League focused mostly on promoting job opportunities for blacks. In the words of one cynical League official, "We provided 'good niggers' for accommodating white employers." Occasionally the League tried to correct minor wrongs. Its tactics were quiet, reasoned discussions with powerful people and with offending employers. Only occasionally, and only after lengthy and unsuccessful discussions with a particularly obdurate employer, did the League take legal action to achieve specific ends. This was a last resort, undertaken quietly and without fanfare or public accusation. The usual method for getting things done was quiet and discreet appeal to the good instincts of others.

There is a bewildering variety of voluntary organizations, some operating much like the National Urban League in earlier times, others employing voluntarism in the fashion suited to their temperaments and purposes. Most are considerably less visible than the familiar ones: churches, labor unions, and the bigger foundations. Even a brief list of the others is long—professional associations like the American Medical Association and the American Institute of Architects to establish and enforce professional qualifications and secure the interests of its members; specialized educational and cultural societies (from symphony associations to the American Academy of Science) to raise funds and encourage professional development; charitable associations like hospital societies and associations for the blind; fraternal organizations like the Masons, Knights of Columbus, Lions, and American Legion, whose activities range from providing college scholarships to taking care of the aged; and specialized groups like the National Urban League, the Legal Aid Society, Consumers Union, the American Friends Service Committee, the Society for Crippled Children, the American Cancer Society, the Farmers Union, the Society for the Prevention of Cruelty to Animals, the Carnegie Endowment for Peace, the Association for Retarded Children, the United Jewish Appeal, the Foreign Affairs Council, the Society of Colonial Wars, the National Rifle Association, and even the Association of Czechoslovak Sportsmen Abroad. The tools of these organizations are persuasion and reliance on people's sense of duty or obligation. This is the source of their strength as well as their weaknesses.

The importance and power of voluntary organizations are anything but trivial. In America in 1970 there were some 3,000 voluntary national organizations devoted to the performance of tasks that altogether involved annual expenditures probably in excess of $2 billion. If the approximate value of unpaid volunteers is included, the expenditures probably approached $5 billion. This does not count bequests and grants by such foundations as Ford, Rockefeller, Guggenheim, and the like. Even in relatively specialized areas these grants were, in absolute numbers, huge. For the performing arts alone, for example, between 1965 and 1971, the Ford Foundation gave $109 million and the Rockefeller Foundation $15 million.. In 1971 corporations gave $56 million to the arts and individuals $500 million.[1]

Besides the national organizations, there are countless local ones. Some have hardly any budget but still perform useful if not exactly urgent functions. Typical examples are Garden Clubs that beautify local streets with seasonal plantings, voluntary mothers' groups that provide free day-care centers for deprived families, hospital auxiliaries that assist in patient care, voluntary father groups that provide surrogate parenthood for orphaned boys, and so forth.

Although the Third Sector is not conventionally thought of as a separate sector, it has by no means been ignored by scholars or men of affairs. There is a vast literature that describes, taxonomizes, and analyzes its various forms.[2] This literature, as well as common observation, tells us that nothing characterizes the Third Sector so much as its enormity, its fragmentation, and the energetic dedication of its numerous participants. Each entity diligently grinds its own ax, often elevating above everything else the importance of its own special cause. Sometimes the cause is narrow, like veterans' rights

---

[1] Howard Klein, "Who Subsidizes the Arts in America?" *RF Illustrated*, February 1973, pp. 4–5.
[2] This literature has been exhaustively summarized by Constance Smith and Anne Friedman in their book *Voluntary Associations* (Cambridge, Mass.: Harvard University Press, 1972).

or doctors' privileges. Sometimes the cause relates to a broader segment of society, as with drives for more consumer information or voter registration. But always the distinguishing operating mechanism—the organizing principle—is voluntarism. In a society whose institutions generally derive their sanction and power from commercial achievement or public law, Third Sector institutions stand out for their dependence largely on the personal dedication and voluntary efforts of their members.

To argue that these Third Sector organizations are somehow less important than the other, more homogeneous sectors would be to miss the crucial point of their social purpose and general consequences. It may be true that the New York Junior League, even with all its good works, is largely dedicated to the narcissistic social climbing of its members and pays more attention to ceremony and status than to serious service. But this cannot be said of the National Urban League, the United Auto Workers, the Cerebral Palsy Foundation, Mt. Sinai Hospital, the Fraternal Order of Eagles, or even Garden Clubs. Each seriously does things that need doing. Each changes people's lives, largely for the better. Nobody can seriously assert that they are socially incidental or peripheral. Without them, important and necessary social tasks would remain undone. This seems obvious enough for hospitals, unions, and the like. But Garden Clubs?

It is an American perversity to view aesthetic institutions like Garden Clubs and fraternal organizations like the Eagles as socially peripheral. Even the National Urban League and most private foundations are rather casually viewed as lying outside the mainstream. It is true that many Third Sector organizations consist of private individuals gathered together only for personal satisfaction and fellowship. Yet people, through associations with, say, Garden Clubs, satisfy personal needs and thereby become more fulfilled and valuable members of our society. The cumulative result may be a less hostile and more satisfying society. Third Sector organizations also perform public tasks that raise the general aesthetic level of everybody's surroundings. To say that such activities are not important is like saying national mental health is not important, or that it doesn't matter what our neighborhoods look like or how dirty our city streets are.

The voluntarism that characterizes the Third Sector lacks, by definition, the kind of binding solidity and continuing stability we commonly ascribe to business and government. But a social institution is no less real or effective—or even necessarily less durable—merely because it is a voluntary association operating without the adhesive bonds of law or economics. Indeed, even businesses go out of business, and though it has law on its side, in America not even government is safely immortal. In spite of government's growing involvement in all affairs, our preferred slogan remains, "That government which governs least governs best."

Still, this very dictum acknowledges that our society needs at least *some* amount of government, however minimal. Our true priorities may have been expressed by

Calvin Coolidge: "The business of America is business." In the end, the American habit is to regard business as the only really legitimate functional institution of our society. All else occupies a lesser status.

Yet without the Third Sector, major tasks that clearly need doing would not get done and major groups in society that clearly need special representation or help would go without it. The very fact that Third Sector organizations are abundant and thriving is testimony to their necessity. They did not materialize accidentally or by immaculate conception. Somebody thinks they are worth the effort. Since that is the case, we have no basis for considering them any less legitimate than business or government. The point is not that their mere existence establishes their legitimacy and worth. The point is that their existence and endurance suggest the presence of a persistent need.

Nor are Third Sector institutions merely dependent organisms that exist only because other sectors provide a facilitating context. If this were so, it would also have to be said that the private sector is a dependent organism: it could not exist without the facilitating context provided by government—laws that bind private contracts, police protection, orderly economic arrangements. The point is, everything is related to and dependent on everything else. All three sectors are bound inexorably together in a benign synergy. Each sector in some way depends on the others, and each is integral to society.

Thus, without the Third Sector we would have a different and less effective society. It is beside the point to say that the organizations which comprise it are highly fragmented, largely voluntary, special-purpose, and often self-serving in the narrowest possible fashion.

I have already pointed out the enormous diversity of Third Sector organizations. Just as businesses and governments differ in function, size, management styles, resources, disciplines, and purposes, so do Third Sector institutions. However, one thing that Third Sector institutions usually have in common is their operating style: social or moral pressure used in support of the technology of persuasion by voluntarily associated members.

That is how they are usually, but not always or entirely. Take labor unions. Unions qualify as members of the Third Sector. In spite of union-shop contracts (and even illegal closed-shop side agreements), America's labor unions are essentially voluntary associations. Their ultimate strength is their power to employ the strike, but not without the membership's voluntary agreement. If unions were to vanish, our society would be different, but discernibly less functional.

The operating style of unions—the way they get some of their major tasks done—is instructive as an example of the evolution of Third Sector organizations. They do their work not entirely by persuasion or social or moral pressure. Unions threaten to and often actually do withhold their labor in order to get their way. They sometimes force workers to join a union and pay dues as prerequisites to their employment. In the early stages of a union's life, violence can be quite common. In time more benign, mutually acceptable relationships develop. Often the relationships become so inoffensively ritualistic that instead of carrying clubs to keep out scabs, strikers carry transistor radios to keep up with the baseball scores. They appear on picket lines in small numbers and on scheduled shifts, to make a peaceful, symbolic show of solidarity and resistance.

The evolution of social organizations from violence and coercive confrontation at the outset to restrained pressures and persuasion in maturity is familiar. Today's labor unions in America work largely with the tactics of maturity—persuasion in the main, with peaceful strikes at times of contract expiration and only occasional aberrations like violence or "unauthorized" work stoppages.

In general, the labor union in America is an entrenched institution living peacefully side-by-side with its putative adversaries. Both the United Steelworkers Union of America and the United Automobile Workers are continuously involved with their employers in joint work-standards studies. These studies, which have been firmly agreed to in binding contracts, are designed to set and periodically modify production rates and piecework pay.

Of course it is more than degree that separates labor unions from such organizations as the old National Foundation for Infantile Paralysis. Indeed, the similarities have often been greater than the differences. Participation in the latter was also sometimes compulsory: frequently the foundation got its revenue from "voluntary" automatic payroll checkoffs during Community Chest and Community Fund drives. But on the whole the National Foundation used social and moral pressure much more often than labor unions do. It kept itself alive by appealing to the public's sense of community, charity, and duty. The unions, by contrast, appealed more generally to self-interest. Still, there is no place in the conventional taxonomy for unions in either the private or the public sector. They belong in the Third Sector.

The fact that a Third Sector institution may have a formal administrative structure and a paid headquarters staff whose operating style is indistinguishable from that of business or government bureau does not disqualify it from Third Sector status. Nor does an organization automatically qualify as Third Sector just because it is formally chartered as a nonprofit institution. A university may have a nonprofit charter, and though its faculty may not have exactly the same motivations as employees of, say, the Westinghouse Learning Corporation, it is still not essentially an association of purely voluntary functionaries. It sells a service for a price, just as do training schools like the RCA Institute or the John Robert Powers Finishing School. Similarly, though the RAND Corporation, the Hudson Institute, the MITRE Corporation, and the Battelle Memorial Institute are organized as nonprofit corporations, they operate just like any other business firm and offer products and services at recognizably businesslike prices.

Some organizations pretend to be Third Sector but have come to deal more in commerce than in community service. The Farm Bureau Federation started out as an association of farmers to lobby for its members' interests. It still does this, and with organized, professional zeal. On the surface it parades as a Third Sector organization of pristine purity. In reality, it is something quite different. During 1969 congressional hearings on proposals to reduce the oil depletion allowance, the Farm Bureau Federation opposed the reduction in the name of its 200,000 members—presumably because the reduction would cut the income of farmers who had sold oil rights to commercial firms. What the lobbyists did not say is that the Federation itself (not its farmer members) had assets of over $400 million in the oil and gas producing, refining, and distribution industries. Similarly, the Federation opposed certain federal controls on the agricultural use of chemicals on the grounds that these would reduce the productivity of its members' acreage, neglecting to mention that the Federation itself operated multimillion-dollar businesses in herbicides, pesticides, and fertilizers. The Farm Bureau Federation has business assets of over $4 billion. If it were correctly classified as a business, it would be equivalent in asset size to the thirteenth ranking firm on *Fortune* magazine's list of the nation's top 500 manufacturing corporations, larger even than Du Pont and Westinghouse. While the Farm Bureau Federation's membership is voluntary, and its supposed purposes are the betterment and protection of its voluntarily associated members, it has obviously crossed over into the private sector.

This does not mean that a Third Sector organization automatically crosses over when it provides services and benefits ordinarily associated with business or government. The Benevolent and Protective Order of Elks is a case in point. In 1868 in New York City fifteen actors, entertainers, and others associated with the theater established the Elks as a social club to provide community facilities and a social gathering place. By 1970 it had grown to a membership of over 1.3 million persons from all walks of life. But the Elks has provided more than easy fellowship. For years its members got solid financial benefits, mostly payments for sickness, death, and burial. That explains why most of its new members used to be family men in their middle years of life. One of life's strongest motivations, especially in a man's later years, is to make provision for his family against serious adversity.

The Eagles, another fraternal organization, had a similar program. Between 1898 and 1940 it paid out over $10 million in death benefits to some half a million members. Obviously the Eagles in that period became an insurance company, as did the Elks to a lesser degree. The Farm Bureau Federation also pays death benefits via formal insurance programs, but it is in no way like the Eagles (which, incidentally, no longer pays these benefits). The FBF has become a business conglomerate, whereas the Eagles continues to function largely as a fraternal organization. It meets its members' basic, day-to-day needs for fellowship and recreation, needs that are not conveniently provided for by either the private or the public sector.

H. L. Mencken was fond of repetitively treating

organizations like the Elks and Eagles as desperate associations of mindless boobs. To agree with that assessment is to speak out of ignorance, arrogance, or the security of one's own affluent, well-insured life. The memberships of fraternal organizations declined after the growth of corporate pension programs and health insurance programs in the 1920s and declined further after the passage of the Federal Old Age and Survivors Insurance Act in 1938. This confirms, as nothing else could, their real importance for so many people for so many years. Their resurgent growth since the 1950s suggests that another of their functions has become particularly important: for millions of people they provide the sense of community that our fragmented society and mobile lives otherwise deny to them.

Those who are deeply involved in its organizations certainly do not view the Third Sector as a peripheral agglomeration of do-gooder and fun-and-games organizations that the larger society merely tolerates and indulges while it is busy doing more important things. For both its members and others, the Third Sector is as central and essential a component of society as the private and public sectors. The fact that so many Third Sector organizations apparently lack rigid, formal structures, the fact that they are so obviously diverse in character and purposes, and the fact that they are so apparently fragmented are unrelated to their importance or effectiveness. What counts is that they are purposeful voluntary organizations that perform vital tasks (vital to either their functionaries, their members, or the whole society) and that affect the social process. They are clearly a discrete and powerful force of their own. The Third Sector is not a fifth wheel, not a random or chaotic assortment of peripheral or lesser institutions. It is essential, and here to stay.

In recent years some of the Third Sector's functions have been taken over by business or government. This testifies to the historic importance of many Third Sector institutions. Government and business have finally recognized the essential nature of some tasks traditionally handled by the Third Sector. As noted earlier, Old Age and Survivors Insurance has displaced the original purpose of many fraternal clubs. Medicare, cortisone, and Mutual of Omaha have reduced the work of the Menorah Home and Hospital for the Aged and Infirm.

The fact that the private and public sectors have over the years supplanted and supplemented many of the more clearly economic functions of Third Sector organizations, does not mean the Third Sector's historic importance has declined. One gets some idea of its continuing usefulness and importance by looking at its less visible work. Civic clubs and lodges are a particularly good example. Wooster, Ohio has a population of only 18,000. In 1970 its Lions Club spent $1,200 on eye care for the poor. The Rotary gave $200 to the crippled children's fund, $1,000 for special meals for the aged sick, $1,600 for flood relief, and about $2,000 for international student exchange programs. (It also supplied funds for 4-H Club activities and created a trust fund for "a worthy Wooster project.") The town's Kiwanis gave

$500 for Christmas presents for needy children, $500 for anti-drug literature for high school students, and $3,500 for college and summer camp scholarships. The Jaycees contributed $200 for a crafts center for the aged, $1,000 for medical aid for poor children, $3,500 for a small factory operated by young people, and $4,000 for teenage tennis and golf tournaments. All the money was raised and most of the work was done by volunteers. Nobody who benefited rose to proclaim the clubs' redundancy or triviality.

The traditional Third Sector organizations described in this chapter comprise what may be called the Old Third Sector. The major purposes of these groups run the gamut from professionalization of their membership (e.g., the American Medical Association) to individual rehabilitation (e.g., Alcoholics Anonymous). Their source of funds is almost always voluntary contributions or dues of voluntary members. Though most have professional staffs, much of the day-to-day work at the local level is done by volunteers. Their operating style—that is, the tactics they employ—is almost always some mixture of persuasion, lobbying, education, and direct aid given by volunteers (such as the work of members of hospital auxiliaries who function as nurse's aides).

Most people who participate in Third Sector activities do so as a genuine act of social service. For some, however, such activities serve a less lofty purpose. For them, participation becomes a badge of honor. Others of social aspiration and privilege behave as if their rank and position make it obligatory to be visibly active in charitable causes. In some cases the visibility is more important than the activity. Social position is affirmed by acceptance into the honored ranks of prestigious charities. Invitations to charitable balls and membership on the more notable public-service committees are marks of social distinction, economic rank, and having "arrived."

But not all Third Sector organizations require of their members only money. Volunteers in these organizations often put in long, burdensome hours of difficult labor and negotiation, make heavy personal sacrifices, and undergo intense psychological pressure. Local fair housing committees are a particularly good example.

In all cases, whether done for pleasure, honor, service, or duty, something that needs doing somehow gets done. Many of society's public- and private-sector institutions overlook things that need doing in society, are incapable of doing them, or are indifferent to the consequences of their own actions and the desires of their own constituencies. The Old Third Sector succeeds in getting some of this work done. It creates with its work a more responsive society.

CHAPTER 4

THE NEW THIRD SECTOR
PUBLICITY AND PUSH

WE HAVE SEEN that the work of the Third Sector has generally been carried on in a quietly restrained and largely unpublicized fashion. Even fair housing groups have worked relatively silently at the local level, preoccupied with zoning laws and an unobtrusive search for cooperative landlords and realtors. The closest these groups have gotten to pushing and shoving is their use of pseudo house-hunters to find and verify discriminatory practices. When they found discrimination, they used their evidence quietly, generally through unpublicized negotiation, to get it corrected.

Now all that has changed. Just as governments have escalated the scope of their involvement in social affairs, and business has escalated its involvement in the affairs of its employees and the community, so now has the Third Sector.

At one time the American government was simply a

traffic manager, taking little active part in society's affairs. Even highways, canals, and fire departments were private, with users paying tolls to their profit-making owners. Today the federal government is an originating activist. It initiates and performs vital tasks that in earlier times were deemed private matters. Business has escalated the scope of its affairs, too. Where once it went to Washington or the local courthouse only to lobby against some proposed legislation or to file a deed, today business goes to the Capitol to initiate programs of its own.

In recent years the Third Sector has also moved up —to new and more aggressive forms of social action. Entirely new Third Sector institutions have arisen. Some are so new that there is not a single word about them in the entire vast literature of voluntary associations. And their tools are equally new. No noblesse oblige or silent persuasion for them. While they have not wholly abandoned persuasion, they now employ vigorous and noisy new confrontation tactics in order to persuade. The Old Third Sector sought largely to soften the abrasions caused by the operations of the other two sectors—by quietly providing aid to the down and out, supporting artistic endeavors for which the commercial system saw no profitable markets, setting aside land sanctuaries for public enjoyment that might otherwise be developed for private gain. Now there is a New Third Sector. It seeks largely to change the institutions which cause the abrasions. It no longer seeks only to respond to the needs or problems of the dispossessed and ignored. It seeks to create a society in which nobody will any longer be dispossessed or ignored. And it uses a new technology, new tools and tactics, to try to get its way.

The New Third Sector is concerned with reform and social transformation rather than merely with "service." When, in the past, pure reform was an organization's only purpose, as in the case of the Women's Christian Temperance Union, it was correctly viewed as a hysterical aberration. Today there are hundreds of such organizations, and like the old WCTU, they do not limit themselves to genteel methods.

To speak today of the "adversary" culture is to employ an appropriately descriptive term. It is not advocacy that characterizes the activism of the New Third Sector so much as adversaryism. Many things are being advocated, to be sure, but these are generally expressed in the form of opposing what is, rather than systematically proposing what might be. The older political agitators at least had the virtue of being programmatic—they wanted public ownership of the means of production, free land, free silver, minimum wage laws, voting rights, free public education, government regulation, retirement pensions, and the like. Moreover, the adversary causes of the past—like those against the central bank, against slavery, against child labor, against trusts —were generally one-shot causes of narrow purposes that emerged episodically from time to time. Never, as today, were they simply one of a throbbing congeries of causes, most of which constantly oppose one thing or another without proposing anything concrete in its place (save a generalized retreat from society or a generalized advance to justice, goodness, love, peace, or public amenities). Today's discontent is a cultural phenomenon —not a discontent with a few isolated social failings, but rather an overall discontent with things and values as they are. The New Third Sector is, in large part, quite literally a "counterculture."

Its most obvious departure from the style of the Old Third Sector is its use of more public, more visible, more agitated, and more impatient tactics. Where the Old Third Sector made a virtue of anonymity and gentle persuasion, the New Third Sector makes a rule of public clamor and pushy pressure. Its tools are loud, insistent, assertive, impatient, and sometimes violent.

At the outset these noisy pressure tools were largely the tactics, if not actually the invention, of the young. But increasingly adults have learned from and copied the young. Middle-class parents roll baby carriages into the streets to keep bulldozers from cutting new highways through their neighborhoods. The aged and poor lock themselves into their slum houses to keep urban renewal from tearing down their homes. Professional women strike and march for women's rights. Professors suspend classes to compel changes in the administration of universities. Policemen, firemen, and air traffic controllers stage sick calls to circumvent antistrike laws. Penitentiary inmates go on hunger strikes. White collar professionals and managers join in boycotts against gun manufacturers and lettuce farmers. Lawyers organize protests against judicial delays. Doctors stage showdowns to force improvement in municipal hospital facilities. Suburban housewives march against escalating meat prices. Blue collar workers demonstrate against bussing their children across town.

The mass demonstrations and other confrontation tactics used by these groups have sometimes produced violence. At times the violence was instigated by the very authorities charged with its avoidance, abatement, and control. To deal with the disorder, new voluntary organizations have arisen to provide independent marshals to keep order and report on illegal and unjust behavior by policemen and other authorities. For a time, everybody seemed to get involved. One organization of marshals consisted of teams of lawyers provided by the Association of the Bar of the City of New York.

New voluntary organizations employing new confrontation tactics have emerged to handle formally tasks that existing institutions do poorly or not at all. Nader's many groups continue noisily to tackle a wide range of public problems. Other organizations using similar new tactics are John Banzhaf III's various groups of Banzhaf's Bandits, which have become the legal arm of a bewildering variety of consumer action groups; societies for the protection of stockholders; associations of retired persons; ecology groups; fair housing organizations; and many others. Even an accredited law school has been established (by Antioch College) around the Banzhaf idea.

A major reason for the New Third Sector's existence is that other institutions and Old Third Sector tactics have not seemed to work. Not even the American government, though increasingly more concerned with the general welfare, has seemed to its many critics to have been properly responsive to the needs and problems of American society. As we saw earlier, government has frequently failed to soften, let alone prevent, the many abrasions caused by the mechanistic workings of the private sector. Nor has there seemed much hope that the problem of unresponsive private bureaucracies can be solved by government bureaucracies.

"Responsiveness" means more than responding to general social conditions and public needs. It also means concern for individual, highly personal problems. Furthermore, as we saw in Chapter 2, the very fact that government must itself be bureaucratically organized and must operate according to an irrepressible bureaucratic logic means that it is not a very promising antidote to the unresponsiveness of private bureaucracies. Government is better suited for other purposes: regulation, control, general economic melioration, and preservation of public amenities. It cannot compel responsiveness, either of others or of itself. Some regulation of industry, some control of certain types of private power, some prevention of the more obvious forms of commercial chicanery—all these are within the fragile competence of government, but, as James Q. Wilson has pointed out, where the self-interest and machinery of opposing institutions are powerful, no power of government can for long prevail. For it to try would be like pushing water uphill: against a law of nature.

One of the distinguishing characteristics of New Third Sector organizations—what makes them largely unique and helps preserve and stimulate their adversary style—is their functional autonomy from the society in which they work. They are usually separated from the machinery and culture of ongoing organizations. Seldom are they interest groups in the conventional sense—groups with common employments, common complaints associated with common experiences, common problems. With certain notable exceptions—such as the Black Panthers, the Southern Christian Leadership Conference, and women's liberation groups—they consist largely of individuals who are *interested* in common problems, rather than being ensnared by common problems. They are not so much intent on solving their own problems as on defining and solving the problems of others—problems hitherto not even recognized as existing. Most have no purpose save the exposure and criticism of allegedly wrongdoing people and organizations, in the interest of opposing what they believe is wrong. In most cases, the affairs in which they are involved do not carry the least whiff of implied social rank or snobbery. The New Third Sector is uniquely manned by people without the slightest aspiration to social position and, generally, without other aspirations of personal power or gain.

The organizations of the New Third Sector have almost no continuing staffs and little money. Everybody works for his particular cause in an atmosphere of urgency and moral rectitude. There is neither time nor money to facilitate the development of the restrained, genteel style and benign astigmatism of conventional bureaucracies. The main reason the New Third Sector can so freely and openly oppose bureaucracies is that its members have no attachment to the bureaucratic culture and its methods. Because they are not responsible for the day-to-day performance of conventional, ongoing tasks, in which efficiency and budgets impose disciplined routines and controls, they develop none of the rigidities that day-to-day routines and emphasis on prescribed performance usually generate. Even when their work requires sustained study and effort, as in the Nader investigations, there is little likelihood of bureaucratic senescence since most of the study teams consist of temporary youthful volunteers who are seldom dependent on their work for their livelihoods. Members of the New Third Sector are independent of those upon whom they focus their insistent attention. They can therefore direct loud, accusatory noises at them without mercy or fear of reprisal.

Thus, it is the combination of goals, composition, and tactics of the New Third Sector that distinguish it from the Old Third Sector and from the private and public sectors. But the main difference is in tactics. The most obviously different tactics are the New Third Sector's intense pushiness, jarring rhetoric, massed demonstrations, moral outrage, and sometimes outright violence. But the tactic that distinguishes it most from the other groups is the calculated reliance on staged, attention-getting publicity. The New Third Sector leans for its effectiveness on the creation of instant TV visibility for itself and at the expense of its adversaries.

The New Third Sector's success is almost entirely due to its mastery of this tactic. The youthful members of the New Third Sector have been well trained by the advertisers whose commercials they have watched on television since childhood. Like commercial advertisers, they show a clear, perhaps even intentional, tendency to overstate every case they make, to overdramatize every issue they discover. The tactics of exaggeration, in both word and deed, get attention, sharpen issues, and stir respectable officials and organizations into some sort of responsive action.

When Ralph Nader said that if an organization is going to be responsible it has to be insecure, this was more than a militant call to arms. It was a sharp observation about how large organizations behave. Nader has seen that his tactic of hovering constantly in the shadows ready to make some plausibly documented accusation to the press quickly gets attention and produces a response from his adversaries. The tactic works. At the least it gets attention; at the most it produces corrections. Thus the Black Panthers have been more successful than the National Urban League in drawing attention to racial problems and getting corrective action. Women's liberation has done more for its cause than the American Civil Liberties Union, the Environmental Action Coalition more than the Audubon Society. Each of these new, relatively unstructured groups owes its success largely to the enthusiastic (and sometimes indiscriminate and unfair) use of media guerrilla tactics designed specifically to catch public attention via the generation of embarrassing publicity.

Neither business nor government has been able to ignore this new brand of sudden, widely publicized criticism. And the media, whether they want to or not, cooperate. The value of the media space (as measured by advertising space costs) that *The New York Times* allots to news stories about New Third Sector organizations is vastly greater than the space it allots to Old Third Sector organizations dedicated to similar causes. In a brief sampling period in 1970 the National Urban League got $6,202 worth of editorial space, the Black Panthers $39,060; the American Civil Liberties Union $10,040, women's liberation $22,792; the Audubon Society $147, the Environmental Action Coalition $1,638.

The tactic of sudden and unexpected public embarrassment, employed by organizations so different from traditional voluntary groups, is a profoundly new phenomenon. If things must have a birthday, for the New Third Sector it is May 3, 1963; the place, Montgomery, Alabama. Here Martin Luther King, Jr., apostle of nonviolence, enlisted confrontation tactics borrowed from Gandhi. King's early mode of bargaining featured moral suasion and dramatic appeals to conscience. On May 3, 1963, he implemented a well-planned provocation that quickly became a model for many other contemporary American activists.

In his celebrated "Letter from a Birmingham Jail" in April of 1963, King rejected the proposal of eight

Birmingham clergymen to negotiate his demands with Birmingham's officials. Nonviolent direct action, he wrote later, must first "create such a crisis and foster such a tension" that meaningful negotiations would be assured. He proposed systematically to violate "unjust laws" on such a massive scale as to "fill the jails." On May 2, King enlisted school-age children in unauthorized traffic-stopping marches. More than a thousand young demonstrators were jailed. On Friday, May 3, in a dramatic confrontation, "Bull" Conner, Birmingham's lame-duck Commissioner of Public Safety, turned loose his police dogs, high-pressure fire hoses, and cattle prods on the massed demonstrators. The cameras of network television reporters, who had been carefully alerted beforehand, whirred away. That night millions of Americans, during their dinnertime TV news, were shocked and outraged at the brutality that tumbled out before them in their distant, peaceful homes.

For four more days disorders raged, on again, off again. On Monday, May 6, a thousand black demonstrators were jailed. A black woman was dramatically photographed being violently forced to the ground by five white policemen. Dick Gregory was arrested. On Wednesday a moratorium on demonstrations was finally declared, and on Thursday negotiations began. Each day the television cameras and newspaper photographers broadcast a running account of an uneven struggle, featuring official brutality, for the horrified consumption of 40 million American television watchers. There for all to see were outrages that some had vaguely known about and most had simply ignored, outrages that syndicated columnists and professional speechmakers had impotently publicized for years.

Earlier demonstrations staged by King, such as the ones in Albany, Georgia the previous summer and fall, had been widely ignored by the nation—owing, one suspects, to Albany police chief Laurie Pritchett's restrained handling of the incidents. But in Bull Conner, King had a known racist and notorious hothead. As King later said, Conner had precisely those characteristics which qualified Birmingham for the new tactics he wanted to try.[1] The following spring the Civil Rights Bill of 1964 was passed. Its passage confirmed President Kennedy's earlier comment to King: "Our judgment of Bull Conner should not be too hard. After all, in his way, he has done a good deal for civil rights legislation this year."

But what the average viewer saw on television was less important than what the new social activists saw. They saw the nation's overnight outrage. They saw the resulting legislation. And they quickly gauged the meaning of these events: the way to get results was to get instant visibility through television. Television goes for photographable action. When the action involves truculent physical encounters between contending groups, so much the better.

Confrontation as a tool of social action swept the land. It was quickly and broadly adopted by anyone

[1] See Martin Luther King, Jr., *Why We Can't Wait*. New York: Harper & Row, 1964.

who had a cause, some nerve, and some organizing skill. It became a favorite mode of organizations like the Southern Christian Leadership Conference, the Student Nonviolent Coordinating Committee, and Students for a Democratic Society. Welfare mothers sat in, peace groups protested the Vietnam war in massed symbolic actions, ecologists "redistributed" trash to courthouse steps, blacks "redistributed" the wealth to themselves in ghetto riots.

The New Third Sector had found a tactic that gave almost any cause instant visibility—often on a national scale. Previously, the Old Third Sector had sought to make large organizations humane and socially responsive through persuasion. The new activists viewed the usual response—the creation of new or extended bureaucracies to do the job—as futile, if indeed there was any response at all. Now what became the New Third Sector saw a possibility of getting the job done via entirely new means. They saw that the tactics of confrontation and publicity generated more immediate and effective responses from business and government than politer tactics ever had in the past.

Confrontation tactics catapulted into disproportionate prominence groups and causes that for years had remained anonymous and impotent and conferred upon these groups and causes enormous power.

The visible use and effectiveness of these tactics also generated even more New Third Sector groups, composed largely of people who became persuaded about these instantaneous-action ways of fighting city hall. Some of these groups, like Ecology Action, were totally new, emerging from nowhere. Some were splinter outgrowths of existing groups—dissident factions advocating harsher and more direct tactics than those the traditional leadership approved, like the old Weatherman faction of the SDS. In some cases the availability of confrontation tactics completely transformed an Old Third Sector institution. For example, the National Urban League quickly shifted from quiet negotiation and persuasion to vigorous public agitation.

Such transformations are not new in public affairs. As I have already mentioned, over the years the American government has changed from being a benign traffic manager to being an active creator of traffic. Instead of being merely the guardian of public safety—making the rules by which others play and helping enforce those rules—government has become an active participant in the game itself. It builds dams, runs electric utilities, operates national mortgage banks, operates gigantic national insurance and pension plans, and the like. Similarly, over the years American business has moved away from its early public-be-damned attitude and has come to give more recognition to the feelings and needs of its employees and customers. Business increasingly provides its employees, both on and off the job, with benefits like safety shoes, cafeterias, sickness benefits, pension plans, educational subsidies, and in a few cases even sabbaticals. For its customers it provides postpurchase repair services, accepts the return of merchandise with no questions asked, and often provides detailed information about product composition and ingredients (some companies did this even before recent labeling legislation).

So it is not surprising that the Third Sector has also changed. The old tactics of restrained persuasion and dependence on the ultimate good will and humanism of men in power seem, at least for the time being, dead. Impatience is in the saddle: impatience with gradual change and normal negotiations. Rational persuasion and gentle nudging have been supplanted by noisy demands and relentless shoving. Space-age media tactics have replaced the simple, paleolithic hand tools of social rationalism.

Of course, "rational" tools will continue to find work and usefulness, but when it comes to big tasks the impatient new confrontation tactics seem generally to be preferred. They have been found too effective to be abandoned. And the more often the new tactics succeed in getting their way, the more often they will be used by new groups with unresolved grievances against what they (often correctly) believe to be unresponsive bureaucracies and an apathetic public.

These tactics are transforming our society. The pattern is already clear; the current is already running strong and wide. More and more often, confrontation tactics are resorted to by totally unexpected people in totally unexpected places in support of totally unexpected causes.

As good a measure as any of the strength and width of the current is what happened in October 1970 in the fashionable Riverdale section of New York City. During a strike of building-service employees, residents in one luxury apartment building became enraged at having to do without hot water. Some of the tenants, who were paying up to $800 a month for their apartments, stormed through the lobby ripping up rugs, smashing furniture and windows, uprooting potted plants, and tearing off wallpaper. Within two days the startled owners settled with the strikers and hot water was returned.

This was not simply a case of traditional Upper Bohemian iconoclasm, nor was it another example of what Tom Wolfe called radical chic, a kind of fashionable slumming of the "in" crowd. It was an example of one segment of the Establishment utilizing a tactic used mostly by the radical Left ("trashing") to compel another Establishment segment to do quickly something that it otherwise would probably not have done at all.

There are abundant examples of the new current. Just five months before the Riverdale incident, Robert Roosa stood on a crude platform mounted in front of the Wall Street Journal building in New York, making a heated speech against the Vietnam war and its supporters in the business community. And Roosa is no wild-eyed radical. On the platform he was an impeccably tailored general partner of Brown Brothers Harriman & Company, one of the most prestigious and respectable of Wall Street's investment houses. Furthermore, he was making the speech at the second Wall Street rally against the war within a week. And although a speech is not like ripping up rugs, considering its tone and source it may be viewed as Wall Street's equivalent of Riverdale's elegant trashing.

Nor are these episodes merely dated or special cases. In the spring of 1973, we saw phalanxed housewives marching noisily against meat prices. In Boston over 5,000 white parents from blue and white collar neighborhoods gathered with bullhorns and giant, televisable signs in City Hall Mall to protest for three agitated hours the forced bussing of their children into schools in distant neighborhoods.

When defined in terms of its social tools and tactics, not in terms of its life style or even of its visible rage, the "adversary" culture today extends all the way from the inner city to Riverdale and Wall Street. Assertive criticism and impatient, nonnegotiable demands are the current mode of social action—not just in America but also in other industrialized and urbanized nations.

It is not pure taxonomic convenience that led historians to define the geologic ages according to the tools of the times, or whimsy that led them to speak of the Romantic Age and the Industrial Revolution. It is no accident that Peter Drucker speaks of "the age of the knowledge worker" and Zbigniew Brzezinski of "the technocratic society." In each case it is the tools of the time that provide the most vivid and helpful description, whether the tools be tools of economic labor (as with the geologic ages and the Industrial Revolution) or tools of inquiry (as with the Romantic Age and the knowledge/technocracy society).

Although confrontation is the most striking tool of

the New Third Sector, its combination of confrontation and voluntarism is of course not entirely novel. Many groups of the past—whether they were advocates of a cause or adversaries against a condition—also employed these tools. This can be said of America's colonial Minutemen, the Mollie McGuires, the Industrial Workers of the World, the early Populists, the women's suffrage movement, the antidraft movement during the Civil War, the prohibitionists, and the Steel Workers' Organizing Committee in the 1930s. Violence in word and deed has been a staple feature of America's radical tradition.

But several things make today's confrontation tactics unique. First is the rhetoric of moral outrage—the New Third Sector's attitude of superior moral virtue. Second is its impatience—its demands that society respond instantly with massive reparations. Third is the frequent use of massed demonstrations and the exploitation of the mass media to get total visibility and quick response. And finally, the very ubiquity of these tactics is unique: they cut across all social segments and include in their ever expanding orbit a vast variety of old and new issues. Of course, most New Third Sector groups employ some traditional tactics as well as confrontation tactics. The Student Nonviolent Coordinating Committee uses fund raising; the Afro-American Student Association uses the tactic of education (setting up black study programs in colleges); the Black Panthers educate children in black pride; and the National Law Center institutes class actions and uses other judicial devices. But the socially significant facts about them lie in their new methods and their total ubiquity.

To appreciate the immense novelty of the New Third Sector, one need only recall its coruscating early years—the endless flow of news and television reports of mass meetings, marches, noneconomic strikes, mill-ins, sit-ins, noise-ins, trash-ins, fires, defacings, bombs, and the outraged criticisms of almost everything anybody with any power in America did or did not do. In those days of the New Third Sector's adolescence, there were always carefully worded publicity releases crying out accusations of injustice and wrong-doing.

The tactics worked. Look only at the speedy response of the Riverdale landlord; at the redirection of urban freeways after mothers stopped the bulldozers with their baby carriages; at the appointment of students to standing university committees after mass meetings and classroom disruptions; at the meliorative measures taken in 1970 by General Motors, Honeywell, Dow Chemical, and AT&T in response to pressure from groups like Campaign G.M. and Charles Pillsbury's Council for Corporate Review; at cancellation of military contracts and the elimination of ROTC at universities after the bombs and the strikes; at the improved black-employment practices in Chicago after Jesse Jackson's Operation Breadbasket boycotts; at the revised hiring practices of Eastman Kodak after Saul Alinsky's Community Action strikes in Rochester, New York; at the separation of the Bedford-Stuyvesant public schools from the New York City system after Rhody

McCoy's strikes; at Polaroid's new South African policies after disruptions by a small group of its own employees.

The New Third Sector has also been effective on the legislative front, in spite of the rhetoric and backlash from its opponents. This is clear enough when one looks at the environmental legislation passed despite the early resistance of powerful industrial polluters, the new civil rights legislation, and President Nixon's appointment of Miles Kirkpatrick as FTC chairman in 1970. Just the previous year Kirkpatrick had headed a study group that severely criticized the Federal Trade Commission for its failure to move against questionable business practices. When he put Kirkpatrick in charge of the Commission, Mr. Nixon—the self-declared probusiness president—was responding to something more than the study group. Even more amazing is how quickly such invincibly conservative politicians as Senators Roman Hruska, George Murphy, and John Tower embraced the battle against poverty and hunger in America. A few years ago even to acknowledge the existence of these problems was to risk marking oneself as a dangerous radical.

Something new has happened very fast. Where in the past it took decades, often generations, to change the minds of men (or the policies of powerful organizations, or the direction of a government), today changes take place with breathtaking speed. So fast, in fact, that full-time activists sometimes seem hard put to find new issues to replace old ones suddenly vanquished through reformation.

The impatient newcomers to public affairs seldom appreciate the power of their tactics and the speed and effectiveness with which bureaucracies can actually respond. How remarkably fast things happen can be seen from the case of the General Motors Corporation. I have already referred to "Campaign G.M.: Project on Corporate Responsibility." It was begun early in 1970 by Ralph Nader and was later run essentially by college students. Its object was to make General Motors reform a variety of its practices. It succeeded in getting two proposals on the G.M. annual proxy statement, and these caused such controversy that the annual stockholder meeting in spring of 1970 lasted a noisy 6½ hours. As we have already noted, General Motors, famous for moving with slow and careful deliberation, took action only a few months after its first, brief encounter with the forces of Campaign G.M. A self-policing committee, composed in part of some nonmanagement members of G.M.'s board of directors, was appointed to study the company's efforts in pollution control, safety, mass transit, and minority hiring and promotion. Before the year was out, management proposed the election of Dr. Leon Sullivan, a black clergyman with strong ties to racial activists, to the G.M. board of directors. Within ten months the corporation announced the appointment of Ernest S. Starkman, a distinguished University of California professor with a record of efforts against auto exhaust pollution, as director of its environmental activities.

Although it is arguable on the basis of past experience under other circumstances whether these appointments will achieve the desired results, what is significant is that General Motors, a corporation whose sales are about the same as the gross national product of Sweden, whose employees and their families roughly equal the population of New Zealand, and whose annual outlays are larger than those of the central government of France, actually bestirred itself with some speed and with something resembling honest determination to be responsive to the issues raised. It did not retreat to the accustomed formula of aloof denial, or of impugning the motives and morals of its critics (earlier, it had taken a regretted step in that direction with Ralph Nader). Nor did it take the ancient road of salutory neglect—of simple silence until the furor blew over and was forgotten. General Motors responded in a significant fashion to outside criticism and did so with uncommon speed.

So have other large corporations recently attacked by social activists—though in some cases the responses were more formal than substantive. One reason for these rapid responses is that the confrontations which highlighted the issues made national headlines. With that kind of publicized pressure, it was impossible to remain silent. At the very least, the accused had to issue a press-agentry-phrased denial of the accusations. But seldom did they limit themselves to doing "the very least." The new-style criticism demanded and generally got more.

In the past, similar and even more serious criticisms

had been made of General Motors and other companies without noticeable newspaper coverage. At most, they got buried back among the want ads. Why such headline coverage now and not then?

A fashionable explanation is that the press is now more willing to publicize criticism of powerful corporations and social injustices because there is now a larger audience for it. So many more people are concerned about these problems; so many more feel frustrated by the massive machinery of today's heavily bureaucratized and unresponsive institutions. In short, social criticism sells papers.

This is a good, but not a sufficient, explanation. Today's greater willingness to publicize grievances and discontents has something to do with yet another distinctive feature of the New Third Sector's style and rhetoric as well as with the tactics it employs.

The older social criticism was essentially ideological. Then as now, critics attacked such central symbols of capitalist enterprise as General Motors, such immemorial injustices as racial discrimination, such venerable governmental failings as the somnolent attitudes of the Federal Trade Commission. But these specific criticisms were combined with a general attack on capitalism itself. Not even during the Great Depression of the 1930s when 12 million workers were desperately unemployed, the ravaged victims of a tattered economy, did people take noticeably to the anticapitalist rhetoric. Nobody was ready, even under those appalling conditions, to abandon capitalism in America. Though times were bad, business had little to fear from the ideological radicals of the Left. Anticapitalist rhetoric was considered an alien, anti-American intrusion on domestic affairs.

Now times are good, and now business often responds with surprising quickness to the rhetoric of what is called the New Left. One reason certainly is that the new rhetoric is so different: it is neither ideological nor that specifically anticapitalist. It addresses itself not to the overthrow of economic institutions but to their reform. It invokes ancient American values like justice and fairness—though it does not always do it fairly. With shrill and urgent rectitude it calls for an *improved* society rather than the socialist purging of its offending institutions. Instead of demanding the public ownership of economic institutions, or even their greater social control, or the socialist management of the governmental process, the New Third Sector generally asks simply that they improve themselves in the service of fairness and social justice.

When the New Third Sector demands that "public" members be put on corporate boards or calls for watchdog committees (as in the case of Campaign G.M.), it is generally demanding reform internally or through outside representatives, not through government. If it views the activities of the Federal Trade Commission or the Food and Drug Administration or other regulatory agencies as wanting, its suggested solution (if it provides one) is usually not their elimination but their reformation through the use of public watchdog activities or through new policies. Today's social activists have as little faith in big government as in big business. They have faith, instead, in "the public"—in some sort of outside surveillance or public representation in the offending bureaucracies or power centers.

Much of today's criticism of powerful private and public institutions is effective largely because of its freedom from ideological abstractions and cant. In recent years, the adolescent outrage of the New Third Sector has generally turned to more subtle and studied forms of confrontation than at its beginning. With a more receptive society these tactics now also work, in part because the practices that more and more New Third Sector organizations have come to focus on have become more highly specific and identifiable. This more pragmatic approach is much easier for the press and other media to swallow, partly because it is easier for the public to swallow.

Yet the media's greater willingness to publicize nonideological, nonsocialist criticism is not the only reason the New Third Sector's criticism has been successful. The baby carriage brigades and Riverdale's trashing did not owe their success to their lack of socialist rhetoric. It was their novelty that made them newsworthy. Many other New Third Sector activities and criticisms are also now newsworthy, in part because the earlier, more abrasive tactics finally created an acceptable climate for their newsworthiness. In any case, adversary activities and criticisms are now firmly formalized. They are especially designed to provoke scenes and get news coverage.

Still, it is not always pure newsworthiness that gets the New Third Sector all its publicity. Daniel Patrick Moynihan contends that New Third Sector issues often get such spectacular coverage because the press itself is infested with members of the adversary culture. They have, says Moynihan, elitist ideas about how society, and especially government, should be run. They themselves energetically seek and eagerly print any alleged wrongdoing or plausible idea for change. Moreover, they are biased. They happily publish any accusation without regard to the trustworthiness of their sources, and televise any provocative incident without consideration of the purposes and legitimacy of the group involved. The sensationally revealing 1971 *New Yorker* article on the Black Panthers by Edward Jay Epstein [2] lends some support to Moynihan. Epstein described in irrefutable detail the American press's uncritical perpetuation of Charles Garry's mythically inflated claims of police genocide of the Black Panthers. Before that, police genocide was an accepted and regularly repeated press reference to the awful shootouts of those days.

But while the absence of ideological cant makes today's adversaries more acceptable, and even though (for whatever internal reasons) the press is more inclined to publicize them, the main reason the New Third Setcor gets so much publicity is still because it plans it that way.

---

[2] "Reporter at Large," *The New Yorker*, February 13, 1971, p. 45ff.

Its accusatory rhetoric and many of its public scenes have been carefully designed and staged specifically to get the broadest possible front-page coverage, regardless (in some cases) of the merits of the case or the verifiable facts.

The New Third Sector is a characteristic instrument of its times. Its tactics are shaped by television's intense palpability and its ravenous appetite for televisable incidents with which to compete with the press. The New Third Sector is a society of media freaks, hooked on the media as a tool of social action. Gone is the Gutenberg age of merely making one's point through literal description, or restrained argumentation, or the academic recitation of austere facts. There is a lot of truth to Marshall McLuhan's fashionable catchphrase that the media have become the message.

Before 1970, General Motors stockholder meetings never took 6½ hectic, publicized hours and never were accompanied by constant taunting from large bands of youthful hecklers, many bizarrely dressed to titillate the news photographers. Before 1969, no one with violent intent ever alerted the television networks beforehand, as did the Weatherman (anonymously) before their attacks on the Chicago police with lead pipes and bags of excrement. Their purpose was to provoke the police into violent retaliation that would make headlines and thereby (they believed naively) radicalize the nation. In his appearances before televised congressional investigating committees, Ralph Nader effectively used the medium to dramatize his auto-safety campaign by displaying large statistical charts and incriminating blow-up photographs of gruesome automobile accidents.

The New Third Sector's use of television and newspapers rests on the assumption of man's essential humanity. Man cannot stand for long an accusing mirror held up to his own sinful shortcomings—especially when that mirror has the powerful focus of television. New Third Sector groups create an enormously powerful weapon when they combine an attack on obvious and long-ignored social problems with an outraged appeal to man's humanity rather than mount an ideological attack on the institutions man has created for his own security and work, when they, like Isaiah, use a rigidly moralistic rather than ideological style, and keep the criticism simple, unambiguous, and televisable.

Unlike political parties, successful New Third Sector groups hammer ceaselessly away at one or two concentrated issues, without equivocation and without going off on distracting tangents. Active minorities totally energized behind their special, narrow cause make child's play of the apathy and complacence of inert majorities. Revolutions are not made by majorities. A revolutionary minority seldom succeeds if the majority is firmly opposed to it, but if the majority is only mildly sympathetic or even neutral, success is often assured. Even when an active minority frightens its opponents enough so they coalesce into an effective counterforce, the militant minority usually scores some sort of ultimate triumph. Those under highly publicized attack generally end up making changes in the direction advocated by their attackers. They see this as a way of at least avoiding total loss.

As we saw earlier, aggressive Third Sector institutions are not new to the American experience—and some have been phenomenally successful. In the past some groups tapped issues that propelled them to the highest level of political power. This was the case with the frontier radicalism that finally put Andrew Jackson in the White House in 1828. It was the case with Theodore Roosevelt's election, which had its beginnings in the Populist revolt against the railroads and the trusts, though it metamorphosed later into a more broad-based political coalition. Other aggressive Third Sector movements did not lead directly to political power but produced major reforms or generated new public attitudes that would later facilitate reforms. Obvious examples are the abolitionist movement of the mid-nineteenth century and the muckraking journalism before and after World War I.

Historically, whenever a Third Sector group achieved some public prominence it spawned other, similar groups. One fraternal lodge led to dozens, one labor union to many, one cultural society to others. In recent times, proliferation has accelerated enormously, partly because of the facilitating spotlight of the mass media. Ralph Nader's Center for the Study of Responsive Law was quickly adopted as a model by law students and other youthful volunteers. John Banzhaf III proved himself the nation's foremost entrepreneur in these matters, creating in fast succession at the National Law Center at George Washington University the following organizations: ASH (Action on Smoking and Health); SOUP (Students Opposed to Unfair Practices), mostly relating to advertising; TUBE (Termination of Unfair Broadcasting Excesses); PUMP (Protesting Unfair Marketing Practices); SNOOP (Students Naturally Opposed to Outrageous Prying); and CRASH (Citizens to Reduce Airline Smoking Hazards). Robert Choate started a one-man campaign against breakfast-food manufacturers, and the giant chart of various cereals' nutritional inadequacies that he presented before Congress was eagerly televised and reprinted by the nation's press, starting with a front-page article in *The New York Times*. Choate immediately received offers of financial support and voluntary help from all over the nation, and other groups were founded to look into other food manufacturers.

The whole consumer movement has made great strides since its small, well-publicized beginnings just a few years ago. Numerous consumer protection organizations now flourish all over America, including even a consumer affairs adviser in the White House and storefront consumer advisory offices manned gratis by law students. The passage of a great deal of federal and state legislation came quickly in the wake of all the Third Sector exposés.

The burgeoning of New Third Sector groups that copy the publicized tactics of others is partly a result of the proven success of the tactics. But it is also a result of the tactics' inherent attractiveness. They provide for their practitioners an instant sense of real involvement, the certainty of doing things rather than merely talking about things. The appeal of "doing things"—especially tangible, physical, even violent things—is an ancient American tradition. Violence is actually the rarest of confrontation tactics, even if one counts unintended violence. Confrontation tactics aim to create instant visibility for a cause or complaint, create public embarrassment or difficulty for the accused, and disrupt existing practices and routines. Ralph Nader's tactics are based almost entirely on these objectives. In a generally sympathetic article [3] Julius Duscha described Nader's particular strategy. Nader told Duscha: "I have a theory of power: that if an organization is going to be responsible, it has to be insecure." The way to make an organization insecure is to stage an orgy of publicity that exposes its vulnerabilities. Nader accomplishes this through the tactics of infiltration and exposé of both his government and his business targets. The tactic of exposé is self-evident. The tactic of infiltration works like this: One of Nader's men inside a government agency advises him of the imminent public announcement of a favorable decision on one of his causes. Nader then quickly dashes off a letter to the administrator in charge demanding to know why a decision has been so long delayed. Copies of the letter go to the Washington press corps. A few days later, when the decision is dutifully an-

---

[3] Julius Duscha, "Stop! In the Public Interest," *The New York Times Magazine,* March 21, 1971, p. 4ff.

nounced, Nader gets credit for once again cracking open the bureaucracy. A few incidents like this make bureaucrats quake and corporation executives listen when Nader speaks. Heightening the insecurity of men in power is a confrontation tactic generally more effective than massed demonstrations and certainly more effective than violence. The secret is in the exploitation of the media.

Such tactics are purposefully the opposite of reasoned persuasion. They are, first of all, a show of public power—the power to frighten, alter, energize, disrupt, or bring things to a halt. But disruption and stopping things are by themselves not enough. There must also be a visible display that will attract the media so that the accused will be publicly embarrassed and incriminated. That is the essence of confrontation—the creation of a public or publicizable scene.

In recent years, groups employing these tactics have had enormous influence on the practices and policies of legislatures, government agencies, corporations, and universities—much more influence than is apparent from the outside. Business managers at all levels have become acutely conscious of the "consumerism" consequences of their actions. The hovering presence of consumer advocacy is felt in corporate committee meetings, in board of directors meetings, and among product managers, packaging experts, design engineers, and advertising functionaries. Wall Street is more nervous than anybody. On June 10, 1971, word leaked out that the July issue of *Consumer Reports* magazine would publish an article questioning the usefulness of STP Oil Treatment, the major product of the STP Corporation. That day, STP stock fell nearly six points from its all-time high. The next day a flood of "sell" orders caused a temporary suspension of trading. On the next trading day the stock fell another 14⅝ points. Five years ago few newspapers, let alone Wall Street, would have noticed or cared what *Consumer Reports* said.

Employees and managers within the corporate sanctuary now actually take measures to protect and more fully inform consumers in situations where only a few years ago no such ideas ever entered anyone's mind. So respectable has consumerism become that in some large corporations it has been institutionalized in the form of "corporate ombudsmen" whose function is to represent the public viewpoint. Ombudsmen now reside at Hallmark Cards, the Chase Manhattan Bank, the Michigan Bell Telephone Company, Pan American World Airways, and the Chrysler Corporation. That their jobs sometimes seem to be a new name for what used to be called community relations, public relations, or the customer complaint department is grist for the cynic's mill. The fact is that something is happening, little though some may think it to be. Even big things start small.

In recent years, consumer groups have fought for legislation for improved product labeling and information, clear statements regarding interest carrying charges, weight and measure standardization, and clear nutritional and safety statements. Business opposition has been surprisingly mild. Business can read as well as others how the activists have gained broad public support for some of their efforts. One crusading New Third Sector consumer investigator reports that he received strong private support from the presidents of several of his target companies. They affirmed some agreement with his criticism but pleaded inability to do anything about it because not all their competitors were willing to go along. They argued that if their companies were the only ones to make the advocated changes, sales and earnings would surely suffer—which is exactly what happened early in 1961 when one cereal manufacturer decided to reduce the size of his swollen packages to the dimensions actually needed to contain their contents. The corporate presidents who confessed agreement with their critic stated that they hoped for legislation which would compel all competitors to take the same corrective action simultaneously.

In 1970 there was turmoil in a whole series of annual stockholder meetings, not just G.M.'s. The efforts of Nader and other groups produced almost instant soul-searching in the boardrooms. It also produced a concern with how to handle such meetings better. This in turn spawned a series of corporate seminars and publications on the subject. In December 1970, the American Society of Corporate Secretaries issued two supplementary booklets to its "Guide for the Conduct of Annual Meetings," covering not only security and admissions at meetings and formats for abbreviated agendas, but also understanding the complaints. In January 1971, 150 corporate executives attended a New York seminar on "Managing the Annual Meeting," sponsored by the Practicing Law Institute. One of the items on the agenda was a discussion of how to correct the conditions which the disrupters complained of. In February 1971, the American Arbitration Association, in conjunction with the New York City Chamber of Commerce, sponsored a symposium reviewing the entire annual meeting philosophy in light of the 1970 events. Even the Supreme Court ruled that the Securities and Exchange Commission was not justified in its refusal to approve certain proxy material proposed by the Medical Committee for Human Rights. The material proposed by the Committee had asked stockholders to bar Dow Chemical Company from manufacturing or selling certain products unless the buyer gave assurances that they would not be used against humans. (The proposal was aimed at napalm.)

Government reactions have also been surprisingly swift. Suddenly the Food and Drug Administration switched from its former focus on small companies and preoccupation with trivial matters (like whether an obscure cough syrup really worked) and began issuing complaints and desist orders against giant companies producing popular, heavily advertised products. Similarly, the Federal Trade Commission suddenly found that its budget was not nearly as limiting as it had for so long claimed in defense of its failure to go after big companies with high-volume popular brands.

New Third Sector agitation has had similar effects in almost all other areas it has targeted—civil rights, school segregation, job rights, pollution, land use, high-

way construction, prison reform, trade union apprentice-
ship restrictions, court reform, university governance,
and of course the war in Southeast Asia.

As we have seen, the New Third Sector does not operate
like militant minorities of the past. It uses, either literally
or figuratively, direct shove where others in the past
usually used conventional political agitation or persuasion. Where the Old Third Sector stood independent
and apart from the private and public sectors, the New
Third Sector stands opposed to them. It exists not so
much to supplement what they do as to compel them to
do things differently or do different things.

Though the New Third Sector has been somewhat
hindered by backlash, it cannot be denied that its confrontation tactics work in some fashion. It is doubtful
whether the changes made in recent years in our society
and in public attitudes would ever have happened in the
absence of these tactics. Certainly things would not have
happened as fast. Certainly the venerable, sedate methods
of the Old Third Sector would have been ineffective by
comparison.

Confrontation tactics serve a dual purpose: they not
only seek to embarrass their targets into changing their
practices but also seek to gain public support for what
the group advocates and gain recruits to expand the
group's work. Confrontation is not just aimed at adversaries but also at the quiescent masses, since it is from
their ranks that supporters and activists must constantly
be enlisted. Most people get their information about

society's problems from the daily media—especially television—and the most effective way to translate people's somnolent discontents into active participation is through these same media.

So confrontation is to today's New Third Sector what law is to government and the tools of economic rationalism are to business. It is what makes the New Third Sector operationally distinctive, programmatically effective, and politically useful. But confrontation, even when it finally does good, is not necessarily all good. Its more aberrant and violent forms cannot by any thoughtful observer be comfortably tolerated—even as "the price of progress." Nor does the fact that these forms of protest and activism tend to backfire and ultimately destroy their instigators—as with the Black Panthers and the old Weatherman groups—provide easy consolation. The New Third Sector *does* pose a danger, but the danger lies less in any of its occasional violence than in the unintended consequences of its more tolerable and regular tactics.

CHAPTER 5

THE FRAGILE BALANCE

Things fall apart; the centre cannot hold;
Mere anarchy is loosed upon the world,
The blood-dimmed tide is loosed, and everywhere
The ceremony of innocence is doomed;
The best lack all conviction, while the worst
Are full of passionate intensity.

—W. B. YEATS

FOR MANY PEOPLE in America, Yeats' words sound a responsive chord. The ordinary citizen, no matter how far removed he is from the scene of action, is daily assaulted by new salvos of outraged discontent and fault-finding about things gone wrong in America, things done wrong, or people wronged. It has become the national mode to be actively dissatisfied and quickly critical—at home, at work, and at play.

The New Third Sector has played a powerfully facilitating role in the development and spread of this dour pathology of discontent. The consequences of the New Third Sector are thus not all beneficial. Everything has its price, or at least its dilemmas. The dilemma for America is that the New Third Sector tactics, which seem best able to produce a more responsive and benign society, may also produce a more unstable and malignant society. Ironically, a society that is using the most effective way it has found to better itself can also thereby embitter itself.

The entire society has become suffused with the New Third Sector's abrasive adversaryism. We are fed an unrelieved diet of charges that the nation is shot through with greed, malevolence, injustice, indifference, unresponsiveness, selfishness, and quackery. The population is constantly accused of its own failings and prejudices, and of its complicity in historic injustices. The New Third Sector is full of highly publicized agitation and outrage. Its apocalyptic moralizing paints a picture of an irretrievably corrupt and greedy society dominated at the top by power and wealth, in the middle by mammonistic imitators who aspire to the top, and at the bottom by petty and muscular opportunists out to "get mine" any way they can.

Twenty years ago the nation's villain was at least safely abroad—a foreign and therefore alien adversary, a detectable, anthropomorphic, and defeatable foe. Today, as a consequence of the unrelieved parade of our shortcomings and the sins of our formerly respectable wrongdoers, the enemy is often depicted as a pervasive and insinuating presence here at home, surrounding us, infiltrating us, confusing and betraying us. We are treated to the specter of guilt hovering over men and deeds we always used to honor. We are caught in the web of Pogo's melancholy pronouncement: "We have met the enemy, and he is us."

The dilemma of the New Third Sector is obvious, though not generally conceded. It may be a useful, productive, and even an inevitable form of social organization and action in a complex democratic society. It alerts, directs, and pushes forward for what it and many others think is an improved society. But the tactics it employs to make itself visible and effective may convert the best of good causes into the worst of social consequences.

What makes the eruption of so many confrontation groups dangerous is not their dependence on violence or coercion (the use of these is relatively rare) or their threats or intimidations, but rather the corrosive effect of their continuing agitation on the fabric of our social system. A hundred good causes are not necessarily better than ten. Continual, accusatory exposure of every instance of alleged corruption, indifference, and injustice is not automatically beneficial. The aggressively rhetorical pursuit of benign ends does not necessarily result in their attainment. Today's surfeit of assertions about what is alleged to be so wrong with society has the power to destroy. The social fabric may simply be too fragile to hold up under this unrelieved din of accusation, discontent, and flagellating self-criticism, even if every charge is entirely justified. Thomas Jefferson believed that an informed public is democracy's own best protection, but the cascade of information now flooding the public is not so automatically benign as Jefferson supposed. As with fine wine and beautiful women, a good thing is not necessarily improved by its multiplication.

The accusatory din may finally become too much. Democratic societies are precariously held together by a fragile web of moral sentiments and civil restraints. No one sensibly expects democracies to have completely democratic governing institutions or completely open and responsive political parties. The governed consent to their own governing by politicians who are visibly less than noble, by public institutions that are visibly less than efficient. They will abide a great deal of disorder and inefficiency rather than risk the uncertain whims even of a philosopher king. But not even the most tolerant and long-suffering democratic society can tolerate *all* manner of disorder and inefficiency; certainly not an unrelieved diet for a long time. Nor can it tolerate for long a perpetual stream of self-criticism about its failings. Even when the purposes are humane and the solutions constructive, no society can for long tolerate continuing agitation and unrelenting shove. If the New Third Sector continues to identify and allege with such outrage, persistence, and one-sidedness, the conditions that are inimical to our society, the population at large will in time develop a generalized cynicism about our institutions, an antagonistic distrust of their leaders and ordinary functionaries, and a growing sense of futility about the value of such traditional virtues as self-restraint, patience, charity, brotherhood, forgiveness, and public service. Indeed, the New Third Sector's vision of a corrupt and nasty society may already be making Americans more and more demoralized about their society's worth and therefore even less capable of solving the problems that confront them. The nation may finally become so confused, disillusioned, and fed up that the result will be national neurosis—a contagious loss of faith in our ability to find common ends, to work out the means for attaining them, and to manage ourselves democratically.

This terrible tableau can have several possible endings. One is nihilism and chaos—everybody severing his traditional moorings, racing off rapaciously to "get mine," regardless of the social consequences. The result: an ascending spiral of imitative greed and corruption. Another possibility is oppression and repression—everybody agreeing finally, and forcefully, to silence the noisy discontent.

Nobody asserts that things have gotten all that bad yet. But if there is a chance that the ubiquitous confrontation tactics of the New Third Sector will generate either nihilism or authoritarianism and repression, the unpleasant question must be asked: Is the New Third Sector working against rather than for us? Are the new confrontation tactics more socially debilitating than socially uplifting, and therefore themselves a serious threat to the society they pretend to preserve?

The American society is more fragile and its stability more precarious than one would think from viewing its industrial might. Somehow, politicians have always known this better than most other people. That in part accounts for the deliberation with which they generally approach suggestions for change. Even such a putatively change-prone leader as President Kennedy went slowly.

Contradictorily, he seemed cautious when confronted with the impatience of his young aides. Here is how Arthur Schlesinger, Jr., explained Kennedy's caution:

> I believe today that its basic source may have been an acute and anguished sense of the fragility of the membranes of civilization, stretched so thin over a nation so disparate in its composition, so tense in its interior relationships, so cunningly enmeshed in underground fears and antagonisms, so entrapped by history in the ethos of violence. . . . His hope was that it might be possible to keep the country and the world moving fast enough to prevent unreason from rending the skin of civility. But he had peered into the abyss and knew the potentiality of chaos.[1]

The problem with the New Third Sector is not so much that it wants to make massive changes but that everything it does generates such passionate intensity and strident adversaryism. Few moments are given over to contemplation or acknowledgment of what is going well. No group or organization is immune to indictment —not even the New Third Sector itself. Through its internecine accusations, the SDS tore itself into three warring factions. The Black Panthers rent themselves with fratricide. Women's liberation regularly fragments itself, and no reconciling caucus seems to hold it together. Ecologists who want well-ordered parks fight other ecologists who want virgin wilderness, and both are

---

[1] Arthur M. Schlesinger, Jr., *A Thousand Days*. Boston: Houghton Mifflin, 1965.

fought by community action groups who want factories.

Nobody can escape the constant impression that there is trouble throughout the land, that nothing is right and there is no solitude or peace. Not even the most somnolent citizen can escape the feeling that things are going from bad to worse, that sickness pervades the whole society and order and civility are gone. In the words of Saroyan's repetitive bum at the bar, "No foundation—no foundation, all the way down the line."

Daily newspapers offer a good example of the unrelieved attack on the population's sense of continuity and order, and hence its confidence in the social system. Take this sampling of items from a single newspaper (*The New York Times*) during only a three-week period:

OCTOBER 3—The National Audubon Society loses in its latest effort to stop oyster-shell dredging in bays along the lower Gulf of Mexico. Dredging helps the shipping companies but destroys wildlife. A federal district judge rules that the Society has "no standing" to bring the suit, and states that the problem is the concern of the U.S. Parks and Wildlife Commission. The Audubon Society accuses the U.S. Parks and Wildlife Commission of complicity with the dredging companies.

OCTOBER 4—The depressed West Coast aerospace industry has laid off over 100,000 engineers and scientists in two years. In Los Angeles County alone, 2,683 engineers were collecting unemployment checks in July. Many more have exhausted their benefits. The article reports: "Frustrated and bitter over what they consider their rejection by a nation that depended on them to fill the missile gap, catch up with the Soviet sputnik and reach the moon, engineers and scientists are changing their attitudes toward themselves and society." They are now talking about direct action; members of the Institute of Electrical Engineers were recently sent a flyer that invited them to a meeting and carried the headline "Engineers in Revolt." One source claims that associations like the awesomely prestigious American Physical Society are to blame for some of the maltreatment of scientists and engineers: "They are a special clique between management and a few top scientists who couldn't care less about most of their members. Look at the A.M.A. That leadership really does a job for doctors. When an MD gets a little gray around the temples, he suddenly gets wisdom. A graying engineer is considered just old."

OCTOBER 4—Book review on *The Supermarket Trap* by Jennifer Cross. The book charges that the American housewife is constantly duped, hoodwinked, overcharged, and manipulated by the companies that sell through supermarkets. Cross's analysis of the problem—namely, that the trouble is not insufficient competition but too much competition—attacks a basic American belief.

OCTOBER 5—Lengthy article on the high incidence of commercial fraud in America, especially against consumers. Describes how irate housewives picketing in front of stores have sought to make changes.

OCTOBER 5—In Illinois' Kern County, west of Chicago, somebody has plugged industrial sewers that pollute the river, capped spewing chimneys, left ripe skunks on the suburban doorsteps of company executives, and even dumped river muck, carcasses of fish, rats, and decayed birds into corporate presidents' offices. It turns out to be "The Fox," a surreptitious Kern County zealot of respectable Republican origins who is fed up with the failure of industry and government to stop the mounting pollution in his once pastoral neighborhood. Said he, "I'm just out to stop things that are illegal in the first place."

OCTOBER 9—"A casual sit-in by parents and teachers, an orderly boycott by more than 4,000 students, and the resignation of the acting principal shut down Benjamin Franklin High School in East Harlem yesterday. The school is expected to be closed again today."

OCTOBER 10—News item on Erwin Somigel's new book, *Crimes Against Bureaucracy*, analyzing the extent and methodology of high-level white collar crimes such as embezzlement. The perpetrators are accountants, bankers, and business executives. The sums regularly taken are enormous in comparison with those stolen from personal victims, but "few of the perpetrators are prosecuted, and of those convicted, few are punished with imprisonment." [2]

OCTOBER 11—Concern, Inc., a Washington-based New Third Sector organization, is conducting a campaign aimed at outlawing plastic bottles and packaging made of polyvinyl chloride. Some 200 million PVC bottles were produced in America in 1969. The accusation is that they clog municipal incinerators and produce harmful air pollution in the process.

---

[2] One is reminded that high-level criminality is not a new phenomenon. There is a rhyme from the English Enclosure movement of the eighteenth century that goes: "The law doth punish man or woman / That steals the goose from off the common, / But lets the greater felon loose, / Who steals the common from the goose."

The Bureau of Solid Waste Management in the United States Environmental Control Administration adds that corrosive hydrogen chloride from these containers also damages plants and buildings. The Bureau says that there's not much of a problem with incinerators, though, since only about 10 to 20 percent of municipal waste is incinerated, there are only about 300 incinerators in the country, and besides "75 percent of them are substandard." Meanwhile the executive vice president of the 1,200-member Society of the Plastics Industry says, "We are not trying to dismiss the problem, but we don't think we deserve the kind of notoriety we have been getting."

OCTOBER 11—An organization called Women on Wall Street meets to map a strategy for getting equal treatment for their members. An economist relates how a major bank sent her to a Council on Foreign Relations meeting where she was turned away because she was a woman. An executive of a major bank relates how the bank's 20 women officers were not invited to the annual officers' golf outing. Other topics discussed are a protest being organized by the National Organization for Women and the organization of a Wall Street chapter of Older Women's Liberation.

OCTOBER 19—A report from Los Angeles says conservationists are increasingly taking to the courts because the federal agencies responsible are either not enforcing laws on the books or enforcing them only half-heartedly. A prominent environmental lawyer is quoted as saying: ". . . we've been through the legislative phase in environment and found that the laws aren't necessarily enforced. Now we're coming to the judicial phase, and if this doesn't work, there's nothing left but 'Green Panthers.' " The article

116

reports that some conservationist lawyers are claiming out-right harassment by the Internal Revenue Service through tax investigations of litigant organizations and investigations of the personal finances of some aggressive attorneys.

OCTOBER 23—Feature article on recent prisoner unrest and government responses to prisoners' demands. Between October 1 and October 4 in four New York City area jails, prisoners seeking reform held guards and others as hostages. Of the 12,000 prisoners in these jails, 8,000 were awaiting trial. Thus, according to law, they were innocent but imprisoned. Occupancy was 183 percent above capacity—nearly three men for each one for which the jails were designed. The Fortune Society, an organization of former convicts and others seeking to create a greater public aware-ness of the problems of penal inmates, declares that the problem is "there are no votes in jail." On October 19, after much criticism and complaining and fruitless negotiation with inmates, Mayor Lindsay reactivated the city's Board of Correction, a citizens' watchdog agency overlooking the affairs of the correction commissioner. (The Board of Correction had been disbanded earlier because of the organ-ized opposition of the city's police officers.) Meanwhile, the jailed inmates complained not only of overcrowding and mistreatment, but of the government's failure to hasten court procedures and expand the courts so that they could get a quicker hearing for their alleged crimes. On October 19 the state's chief justice responded by announcing eight adminis-trative steps to alleviate the criminal-case backlog in New York City.

OCTOBER 25—A report that legal services for New York City's poor would be cut back next month because of lack of additional financing from the federal Office of Economic Opportunity. Seven of the city's 26 offices that provide virtually free legal advice to indigent persons were to be closed. There was a mill-in protest that spilled into the streets.

And when it is not the news columns that are flooding the nation with this gloomy parade of discontents, it is the editorial and even the advertising pages. Common Cause, an organization devoted to the alleviation of a broad range of social, economic, and political problems, placed full-page ads throughout the nation declaring:

> Wherever you touch the public process in this country today, almost without exception, you will find a failure of performance.
>
> The air we breathe is foul. The water we drink is impure. Our public schools are in crisis. Our courts cry out for reforms. Race conflict is deepening. Unemployment is rising. The housing shortage has driven rents through the roof. Inflation runs rampant, sapping the initiative of our people and wiping out the life's savings of our senior citizens.
>
> The things government is supposed to do, it is not doing. The things it is not supposed to do—encroaching upon the lives and liberties of its citizens—it *is* doing.

Nor is the New Third Sector the only group that is generating bad news about our shortcomings. The reporting media themselves, competing with each other for attention and fearful of seeming passive while others dig up all the nation's dirt, have become active generators of evidence that things are desperately wrong with our whole society. The style of the new journalism is itself an adversary style. Television focuses largely on visible, photographable action. The press, through investigatory and interpretive reporting, generally focuses on ignored, forgotten, or largely hidden matters. But always the emphasis is on what's supposedly wrong, never on how good things are or on the progress that is being made.

In fact, one of the big problems with the New Third Sector is that it so often sees the enemy as worse than it is. Often people are accused of rapacious greed and irresponsibility when they are only engaged in the normal human quest for personal security. Wrongdoing is asserted when there is only accidental wrongness. Studious and callous indifference is proclaimed when there is only automatic, ancient custom. Diabolical motives are attributed to people for condoning injustices they did not know existed, and for resisting corrections of problems of which they were not aware. As a consequence, many of the accused and vilified feel, justifiably, that they have been mistreated.

Whatever society's faults and failings really are, they have often been magnified into hideously elephantine proportions—a veritable cesspool of greed and corruption, chaos and disorder, duplicity and injustice, indifference and callousness. No wonder the population has begun, for the first time in American history, to lose its optimistic faith in the future. Two days before

America's national elections in the fall of 1970, Tom Wicker (then a Washington correspondent for *The New York Times*) summed up the prevailing feeling:

> The dominant impression of one observer who has roamed the country this fall is more of a mood than of an ideology. A swing to the right is not clearly so evident among the American people as is a pervasive sense of crisis, a widespread feeling that something has gone wrong in America—with the economy, with "the kids," with life in the city society generally, with a war that no one even tries to defend any more, with the way things are and the way people have to live in the most highly "developed" of all 20th century societies.

By the summer of 1973, with the Vietnam war at last over, the other discontents and fears continued—muted in comparison with the terrible tones of 1970, and vastly outpublicized by the Watergate scandal, but still abundantly and vigorously present.

Peter Schrag referred to the American condition as "the malaise that lacks a language." But "malaise"—with its implications of confusion, listlessness, withdrawal, and passivity—is hardly accurate. Even those sectors not generally acknowledged as having much involvement one way or the other in the struggles of our times are becoming increasingly active. Certainly they have become concerned with the issues that the social activists have raised, or with the noisy tactics with which they raise them. The so-called silent majority is silent only in comparison with the New Third Sector's advertised activism. Its talk and concerns may not qualify for urgent headlines, but this doesn't mean they don't exist. Members of the "silent majority" are neither silent nor passive. It is only that they talk, complain, and raise hell largely among themselves rather than in public. The evidence has been poignantly reported by Robert Coles and Jon Erikson in *The Middle Americans*.[3] When they do publicly display their worries and their wrath, the rest of society is surprised and even outraged, as witness the reaction to the head-busting confrontations between muscular, marching hardhats and massed students on Wall Street in May 1970.

The fact that the hardhats are seldom heard from is not attributable to either their satisfaction or their indifference. They simply can't afford to take the risk of raising hell. Ordinary wage earners just don't have all the time for protest that college students and professional activists do. They can't take off to march whenever they get fed up or indignant. It is no coincidence that the hardhats marched on the Wall Street demonstrators during an extended lunch hour. One newspaper suggested a conspiracy between the union leaders and the construction firms, since the men normally got only a half-hour lunch but weren't docked for coming back late from their Wall Street foray.

It is not just that ordinary wage earners have jobs that keep them off the streets. These jobs also make it essential that they keep their names out of the papers.

[3] Boston: Little, Brown, 1971.

For students and full-time activists, getting publicity and their names in the paper is an essential part of the protest strategy. For wage earners with families, it risks losing one's job. Though access to the media exists equally for ordinary wage and salary workers and the young professional activists, the former by comparison simply don't have the easy freedom to take advantage of their opportunities.

The ordinary wage earner suffers a special problem. Besides being told daily by the media what is wrong with the nation and having little power either to improve it or react to the confusion, he is also constantly bombarded with alluring but hopelessly out-of-reach advertising images of what presumably is a "proper" American standard of living. These ads try to create aspirations that expand consumption. But the total inability of so many viewers to satisfy these aspirations also expands frustration and bitterness—especially in view of the continual news stories of others who are reaping the benefits of venality and greed. Reared on the traditional shibboleths of industry, frugality, sobriety, and patriotism, with their promises of just rewards, working-class people see all around them a lot of evidence to the contrary. They see protesters, "welfare chiselers," and U.S. senators with $160,000-a-year cotton-farm subsidies "getting theirs" simply by grabbing. For themselves, they see ruinous inflation, dead-end jobs, and even the "loss" of their children—who often seem to follow alien values in distant places. At the same time, the mass media constantly imply in breathlessly urgent ads an obligatory life style that is beyond the reach of a great many Americans. To cite some statistics, the U.S. Department of Labor declared in 1970 that a "moderate" standard of living for a family of four required about $9,100 a year. Yet at that time the median U.S. family income was less than $8,000. Blacks, of course, are the worst off. Though in recent years their incomes and living conditions have improved faster than those of whites, the overall difference remains so disproportionate that any reasonably compassionate white American can feel only shame over the situation. Still, many white Americans are not so well off themselves. Of white American families, 40 percent earned between $5,000 and $10,000 in 1970. Included in this category were factory workers, storekeepers, small farmers, cab drivers, policemen, foremen, longshoremen, postal clerks, many public school teachers, and many of the elderly—all the people passed over by affluence on the one hand and public benefactions on the other.

Thus the working-class or lower-middle-class white American, not just the black, is uneasily suspended well below the level of affluence, yet he is told that affluence is the appropriate American condition. Though he works diligently at a dead-end job, still somehow believing in the promises on which he was raised, his condition seems to get progressively worse. Inflation robs him before he can spend what he earns. Assorted social planners and white liberals seem locked in a conspiracy against him. They encourage ever multiplying numbers of urban blacks to go after rights and benefits which he seems to be paying for. As blacks move into his lower-middle-class white neighborhood, he sees slashed the value of the home on which he has been making mortgage payments for so many arduous years. The liberal white collar whites move away to the suburbs, leaving him to occupy a racial buffer zone of constant, simmering tension and to pay the escalating taxes needed to finance the expanding big-city government. Under the circumstances, the working man cannot imagine his condition improving. Suddenly the ancient verities of work, frugality, persistence, and sobriety seem to have stopped paying off.

Indeed, everything seems suddenly to have become alien. Everything is disturbingly different. Protesters, agitators, "freaky" college kids, and all manner of New Third Sector groups seem to be systematically tearing away at his traditional faith, constantly spotlighting what's wrong with America, and always getting their way by means of repugnant tactics that, in any case, are not available to him. When he occasionally blows his top and employs precisely these same tactics, as in the case of the Wall Street hardhats or the Boston City Mall demonstration in 1973, the whole fury of the mass media is unleashed upon him. When in desperate frustration this exemplar of the old virtues, long celebrated for his predictable vote for progressive Democrats, thought of supporting George Wallace, he was accused of bigotry and even fascism. It was no surprise that in 1972 he voted for Richard Nixon. McGovern, or at least his followers, represented an assault on all the middle-class values and aspirations that he and most other Americans felt had worked so well in the past.

Today, not even the labor union is available to the wage worker to provide some reassuring sense of shared goals and common values. It used to be that the union met many of the economic, community, and psychological needs of the blue collar worker. In the 1930s, and, actually, as late as the 1950s, organized labor sought to provide workers (especially those involved in mass production) with a sense of special identity that they were unable to get from their jobs. In those days unions also promised some vague assurance that a worker would get a square deal. A square deal then meant being treated right on one's job. That assurance meant a great deal to a man, and therefore so did the union.

Today all that is largely taken for granted, and so is the union. Today, blue collar workers are far more concerned about getting a square deal away from the job. Decent wages and the right to be treated well on the job are reasonably assured. (In fact, a more common problem is whether the union itself treats its members decently.) It is off-the-job rights that now seem in jeopardy—the right to have, after years of diligent mortgage and tax payments, a home that has not been severely depreciated; a neighborhood that has not been robbed of safety, tranquility, and essential services by the intrusion of seeming rabble; income that has not been brutally cheapened by spiraling inflation and by escalating taxes that support people who seem unwilling to work, save, or do their part. That is the new scenario of blue collar urban life as seen by those compelled to live it.

Once unions were considered part of a "labor movement" that was setting out to reshape society. In those days unions were led by exceptional men from the rank-and-file. Today they are led by people who might easily have chosen alternate careers as business leaders. Unions have themselves become big bureaucracies doing routine bureaucratic stuff. In the winter of 1971 the white collar employees of the United Automobile Workers union went on strike against the union for higher wages. Emil Mazey, the union's veteran secretary-treasurer—who had had his head broken open more than once while resisting hired strikebreakers in the 1930s—crossed the picket lines of his union's own employees. Confused and deeply offended, he told a *New York Times* reporter: "I just don't understand. We pay them well. We're like a family. We have office picnics and good times together."

A strike against a big company used to have galvanizing overtones of class conflict and moral purpose (sometimes reinforced by the invigorating abrasions of picket-line violence). It is now merely a routine show of economic staying power, just another form of competition. Picket lines have ceased to be massed displays of worker solidarity. Instead, they are extensions of the job routine. One's turn and place on the picket line are as carefully scheduled as one's turn and place on the assembly line. Where once a certain stoic heroism was attached to walking out on one's weekly paycheck, now union strike funds have removed even that quixotic satisfaction. Old-fashioned union leaders like Philip Murray, John L. Lewis, Walter Reuther, and David Dubinsky used to lash out inspirationally like Isaiah against the workingman's oppressors. Today's leaders are tired old men (over three-quarters of the men on the AFL-CIO's Executive Council are over 70 years of age) who go to fancy-dress dinners at the White House and attend the quadrennial national political conventions to peddle the workingman's vote. Unionizing is no longer an appealing cause, especially not to the young. The International Ladies' Garment Workers Union for years operated an institute to train organizers and other union officials. In 1961 it had to be shut down for lack of promising students. The "union movement" is dead. Not even where most organizing effort is now centered and where most union growth now occurs—in white collar employment—is there any zeal or commitment to the unions people join. They're just another business.

For the worker there are only receding memories of old promises. He has come to suspect that neither industry nor frugality nor postponement of gratification is going to get him very far, and without these values to hold things solidly together, his behavior loses predictability. Things fall apart. When *Fortune* magazine reported on Detroit's problem with uncontrolled absenteeism and "blue collar blues" on the assembly lines, and referred to a new breed of "blue collar rebels" who increasingly resisted the discipline of either the employer or the union, the magazine was talking about a national disorder that not even rising unemployment could abate.[4]

A pervasive restiveness is loosed upon the land, together with a massive erosion of the old virtues of diligence and duty, commitment and continuity, civility and cooperation. Even when the captains of industry and the chieftains of the unions work diligently together, they can't put things right again. There were 38,000 important local issues on the docket of the UAW–GM bargaining negotiations during the big strike of 1970. That was over half again as many as in the 1964 contract talks, and over triple the amount in the 1958 talks. The union locals would not agree to a national contract that the leaders of both management and labor wanted unless it included solutions of their special problems. Since a national contract, by its very nature, could not solve these problems, things dragged on until finally separate local bargaining sessions had to be arranged.

This growing local assertiveness is not just due to differences in local working conditions. It reflects a more profound transformation: "Things fall apart; the centre cannot hold." In the bigger factories of the large cities, guns and knives are staple discoveries in workers' lockers. The old consolidating ethos, whereby men with similar interests compromised their differences so that they might go forward together, has lost a lot of its adhesive

---

[4] Judson Gooding, "Blue-Collar Blues on the Assembly Line," *Fortune*, July 1970, p. 69ff.

power. Workingmen pull apart because all else in society seems to be pulling apart.

One of the deepest and most significant schisms in American society is that between the New Third Sector and the old-fashioned political liberals. The latter share, and for years have worked for, a good many of the goals that the New Third Sector now embraces. Yet the more radical new activists seem to save their severest contempt for precisely these liberals. They are constantly accused of hypocrisy and cowardice—of talking and writing at sterile length about justice, freedom, and economic equality without ever having actually fought for them, and certainly not with direct action, the only method approved by the New Third Sector's more radical members.

Thus old-style political liberals—ranging from traditional social activists like the early CIO union leaders to the more recent white collar activists of Americans for Democratic Action—are suddenly shocked and outraged by the New Third Sector's scorning, scorching attacks upon them for all their diligent years of liberal labor. The new radicals lump the old liberals into a single mixed bag of adversaries, right along with the National Association of Manufacturers, Wall Street, the military-industrial complex, and Mr. H. L. Hunt.

The difference between the old liberals and the new radicals is not just a matter of old wine in new bottles. The wine is also new. For the traditional liberal, everything has come unhinged. Once men who worked for common, compassionate ends placed the greatest value on preserving democratic processes and protecting civil rights while seeking these ends. Today large numbers of people committed to similarly compassionate ends are profoundly divided on the issue of means. The magnitude of the rift may be measured by such spectacles as Nathan Glazer, a ranking intellectual liberal, writing articles on how the tactics and values of the New Third Sector's radical segment have conservatized him irrevocably.

The inability of people with common purposes to work together characterizes all other sectors of American life. Nothing seems to work. For some, the result is despair, futility, and even malaise—emotions expressed in alternating displays of anger, withdrawal, or assertiveness. In 1967 John W. Gardner, the former Secretary of Health, Education and Welfare and head of the Carnegie Corporation, founded the National Urban Coalition, which at its height had some forty affiliates in cities throughout the nation. After three years of trying to bring together such diverse groups as businessmen, union officials, church leaders, and civil rights activists, Gardner gave up. The organization simply fell apart. Gardner then organized a new, more politically active group, Common Cause. Wisely, Common Cause is organized around individual members, not organizations. But even so, progress toward its goals is negligible. It simply isn't activist enough. The nation seems to need more agitated tactics in order to hear what's being said. Meanwhile, the National Urban Coalition has continued on paper, but its local support has all but dried up.

Nobody seems any longer able to work together

for long, even on agreed causes. The SDS tears itself into warring factions. The Black Panthers execute and excoriate each other in a sustained orgy of violent rhetoric and behavior. Even members of the United Mine Workers union fight among themselves until one of their dissident leaders is assassinated. And the American Medical Association loses its monolithic grip as organized dissidents go their special way.

The difficulty of sustaining any sort of cohesion and continuity within groups nominally dedicated to social amelioration is symptomatic of the rapid erosion of the forces and sentiments that bind social systems together—the spirit of cooperation and compromise, fairness and restraint, civility and sacrifice, purpose and dedication. All around him the average American witnesses the decline of these values and the persistent short-circuiting of normal, traditional, fair-minded procedures for getting things done. Orderly behavior and respect seem gone forever. There seems to be no rest or reason, no future except turmoil, dismay, and everybody's self-justified pursuit of his own narrow and uncompromising aims. Increasingly the average man feels himself driven to protective emulation. He'll go out to "get his" because that is exactly what others seem to be doing and getting away with, and because it seems the only way to keep up.

The symptoms are everywhere. The ordinary self-restraints against temptation, which only individuals can impose upon themselves and without which no society can function, are falling into rampant disuse. Pilferage in retail stores by people of all ages and incomes is epidemic. Public libraries in the most affluent suburbs station armed guards at their doors and attach surveillance mirrors on their walls. Escalating burglaries and robberies compel practically every college dormitory in the country to install security patrols. Telephones in the administration buildings at Harvard University are fitted with anti-dialing locks to prevent students from placing calls to California and Paris. Petty traffic violations, such as unauthorized parking and running red lights late at night, are skyrocketing.

A society—like a person—can stand only so much unrelieved self-criticism and self-doubt. The New Third Sector's relentless finger-pointing at shortcomings and mismanagement, its persistent accusations of corruption and greed, have helped stir enormous unrest and cynicism. People trust each other less and less. If this trend continues, the result will be an exponential escalation of corruption and selfishness.

The point is not that society's failures should go unexposed, but that they should be exposed less shrilly and constantly and with some sensible regard for the possibility that they are accidents rather than contrived, and that their continuation reflects cultural lag rather than conspiracy. No complex society will ever be free of corruption, malfeasance, stupidity, and injustice. Perfection is particularly unlikely in a complex and affluent society, where the profits from corruption and malfeasance are high and the possibilities of stupidity are many. The numerous groups that investigate and report on such failures seem almost pathologically inclined to exaggerate the normal quotient of misbehavior and stupidity. As a consequence, they are in danger of creating the very behavior they condemn. Average citizens, outraged by what they are told, are themselves becoming more greedy and corrupt. If this continues, the fragile bond of self-restraint and civility that holds society together may be violently torn asunder.

Most of the accusations and exposures of the New Third Sector may indeed be justified, and there is no doubt that confrontation tactics are useful in this world of complex, bureaucratized institutions. The problem is to get enough prodding criticism and investigation to keep our institutions honest and reasonably responsive while at the same time avoiding the excessive self-flagellation that has made Americans so cynical and despairing.

CHAPTER 6

PROGNOSIS

THE DESIRABLE AND THE FEASIBLE

CLEARLY, the impact of the New Third Sector goes far beyond the immediate redressing of wrongs. Its persistent noise about widely acknowledged problems and injustices can create dangerously unstabilizing second-order effects. While America may be able to withstand these effects, there is a chance it will not. America has no monopoly on stability or order—or even on survival.

Still, any suggestion that America is doomed has an uphill fight against history. It is true that America has strong tendencies toward turmoil and divisiveness, but so do other, even less stable nations. Nervous prophets of the apocalypse have to face the fact of America's historic resilience. The terrible urban riots of the summer of 1967 killed nearly a hundred people. Dozens of city blocks were devastated as if by war. The nation teetered fearfully on the edge of contagious violence. It was a much more somber test of America's resilience than we face today. Yet we survived. It might be argued that any people who can sufficiently tune out and resist the $20 billion worth of obtrusive, crafty advertising that each year urges them to buy ever more goods beyond their means, can also tune out the underfinanced noise of amateurs who seek by less sophisticated means to influence them on other matters.

Only a few social disruptions in America have ever matured into social movements of any profound or lasting impact. All the rest were shrill sounds that developed no real following or self-sustaining power. Even when a new movement gained political strength—as did Theodore Roosevelt's Bull Moose party in 1912 and Robert LaFollette's Progressive party in 1924—even then, things petered out more suddenly than they had emerged. Merle Curti observes:

> From the time of the Populist uprising to the second election of President Wilson in 1916, political, economic, and social reform had been an impressive element in American thought. At the end of the 1920's, however, John Chamberlain, surveying the preceding decades, could entitle his survey, *Farewell to Reform*. Frederic C. Howe, a veteran champion of municipal improvement, struck a note of defeat in his autobiographical *Confessions of a Reformer*. Lincoln Steffens, whose muckraking had been so spectacular, expressed disillusionment with reform and muckraking, and even suggested that America could achieve socialist goals under the auspices of beneficent capitalism.[1]

[1] Merle Curti, *The Growth of American Thought*, 3rd ed. New York: Harper & Row, 1964.

By the mid-1920s the public had lost interest in such reformist literature as Upton Sinclair's *The Jungle* and Jack London's *Martin Eden*. In those years, the book that captured the national imagination was Bruce Barton's *The Man Nobody Knows*, an irrepressibly optimistic panegyric which identified Christ as the prototype of the modern businessman. It was a flourishing best seller for two years.

Many other, more recent movements have also suffered declines. Socialism is a good example. Early in 1970 Michael Harrington, chairman of the United States Socialist party, wrote an article entitled "Whatever Happened to Socialism?" [2] The metaphor was that of post-mortem. He pronounced that in England socialism had become "Tory, genteel, and geriatric." In other countries the old passion has been spent or turned sour, not because its leaders were corrupt or fatigued but because socialists finally came to recognize that "the majority of the people in advanced societies have, at least most of the time, been sufficiently integrated into the system so as to want increments of change and not total transformation." Increments of change, according to Marxist dogma, merely prop up and prolong the capitalist order. If this proves to be true, the future of American socialists will be little different from their past, when they were reduced to talking dialectically to each other in dingy meeting places over tea.

The noisy activists of the New Third Sector, with

---

[2] *Harper's*, February 1970, pp. 99–105.

no sustaining dogma to hold them together, will have even more difficulty keeping alive than the socialists, who at least have an ideology and a messianic historic hero to help sustain their faith.

Like the socialists, the more agitated segments of the New Third Sector are famous for their self-destructive, internecine squabbles. Frustrated by their inability to get fast and sufficient results from an indifferent society, some radicals escalated their agitation and employed increasingly more outrageous means to achieve their alleviating ends. But the escalation was felt more by the agitators themselves than by the society. The Black Panthers were destroyed neither by police bullets nor by police harassment, but by internal dissensions generated by the increasing extremity of their measures and their rhetoric. The Weatherman were not fragmented into warring factions by the president of Harvard University or by the Ohio National Guard at Kent State. They were their own undoing. With both groups, impatience, inexperience, and insensate methods impeded success. The youthful leaders became as incapable of getting along with each other as they were of getting along with their parents and their professors.

This is the special problem of the New Third Sector. Many of its organizations seem doomed to abbreviated lives precisely because they are largely manned by young and inexperienced people who know little about the administration of ongoing enterprises and who, in any case, grow older. When they make mistakes, as all leaders inevitably do, their members, conditioned to speedy action and absolutist modes of social analysis, usually become impatient and dissenting rather than pledging renewed support. Moreover, the leaders, thrust into sudden prominence and exhilarated by the glow of power, soon lose interest in the inevitable details of managing that power. Enticed by other causes which look comparatively easier to conquer, they have a visible tendency to pull away, finally dropping out of what they started—and sometimes out of the society they originally sought to change. Stokely Carmichael moves quietly to Africa. Abbie Hoffman becomes a freaky clown performing for upper-class bohemians at professional prices. Sam Brown, the founder of Ecology Action, disappears tired and disillusioned into an urban commune. The more extreme groups in the New Third Sector do not seem able to survive their own extremities.

Another reason the New Third Sector may be temporary is that it lacks sustaining finances. All the world's voluntariness and moral fervor will not pay for long-distance telephone calls, airplane trips, printing bills, and the inevitable meeting-room expenses—to say nothing of reliable clerical help, which in time wants a salary, not just an appreciative pat on the back.

Even if it were not subjected to the inescapable press of economics, the New Third Sector might disappear simply because its tactics cannot be sustained. Like romantic love, ecstatic involvement is as temporary as it is tempestuous. By definition outrage is episodic and short-lived; otherwise it is madness, which is self-defeating. The members of many New Third Sector groups are hot-headed, impatient, unbending, and self-righteous. It is a style and habit of youth. The young have always been disproportionately unconventional and unstable. They have also always grown up.

The pushy, intemperate New Third Sector can find its historical counterparts in the early New Deal, in the Russian Bolsheviks, in Fidel Castro, and in all the xenophobic new leaders of Africa. It can even find counterparts in the business world: it is the new firms that do the unconventional, irreverent, and impatient things. Witness the activities of Korvette's (in retailing), Donaldson, Lufkin & Jenrette (on Wall Street), and the Leasco Corporation (in computer leasing). The unconventional styles and tactics of new organizations are part of their struggle to be born and stay alive. Once firmly established, they settle into more restrained and predictable "adult" routines.

This suggests a final reason why the New Third Sector may be temporary—or at least why its recent tactics may be temporary. If the New Third Sector organizations obtain adequate financing, they will certainly adopt many of the very same bureaucratic rules and procedures they fight against. In maturity, they may well do what mature institutions typically do— adopt the conventional methods of bureaucratic administration, persuasion, and lobbying (methods adopted, for example, by most of today's labor unions). It is the fear of precisely this that keeps Ralph Nader from organizing his various enterprises along conventional lines, from hiring a badly needed secretary, and from leaving his austere rooming house where he has only a pay telephone. (So far, nobody else has been willing to follow Nader's ascetic example.)

Thus, a number of arguments can be mustered to show that the New Third Sector is temporary, that there is little need for alarm. This suggests that conventional social norms and civilized social attitudes will be preserved because the New Third Sector cannot sustain itself in its present coruscating form. Society is safe.

The truth seems to be that the New Third Sector is evolving, not disappearing. It is not really changing its tactics or attitudes, not itself turning bureaucratic. Some New Third Sector groups dissipate themselves by attacking too many problems at once. Some moderate their rhetoric and their tactics to the point of invisibility. Others redirect their efforts into more manageable causes. The most common fate of these groups is the same relative anonymity that characterizes the Old Third Sector. But meanwhile, other groups and leaders emerge to revitalize the New Third Sector.

And, though the enthusiasm of individuals may wane, the new groups themselves are unlikely to get quickly tired. New recruits constantly come in to provide energy and assertiveness where the will and spirit of others have abated. The best examples of this are the Ralph Nader organizations. Each year more people apply for service, and each year the scope of the Nader activities widens to accommodate the influx of both people and money.

But there has been a change in the New Third

Sector's tactics. Violence, massed confrontations, and high-decibel public outrage have declined. These "hard" tactics have been largely replaced by softer confrontational techniques—but the spirit remains. As long as confrontation tactics continue to work and are allowed by law, new leaders will understandably see no point in switching to something else before they've tried what has indeed worked for others.

The spirit of adversaryism remains too. Lately it is disguised in more conventional styles, but it still whips up a never-ending stream of issues, accusations, and allegations. In America accusatory fault-finding is now an accepted mode of public discourse, and insinuation a routine style of rhetoric.

What some commentators see as "the cooling of America" is merely a decline in the more aberrant forms of social protest. We cannot say the American condition has improved just because, for a stretch of time, no bomb-planter is killed, no policeman has bags of excrement thrown in his face, no university president is locked out of his office, no ghettos go up in flames, no annual meetings are disrupted, and no buildings are trashed. The same issues still exist; they are merely being handled in other, less visible ways.

To verify this, all one needs to do is read newspapers and watch TV, where discontents continue to be regularly and enthusiastically featured. Among the young, the old symptoms of dissatisfaction remain. Well into 1972, the dropout rate at Harvard University was greater than ever. Jesus freaks and demon sects proliferated. High schools became the new theater for the disruptions, which had previously been confined mostly to prestigious colleges. By 1973 the campus activists seemed quieted only because the institutions they had been attacking were now silenced or intimidated. It is a superficial observation to say simply that students now work harder at their studies and are more concerned with job opportunities. Actually, many are deeply involved in the same types of issues as before, and others have retreated into resignation or been engulfed in the cynical backlash that now impels them to "get mine."

Among adults, advocates of environmental protection, women's liberation, consumer protection, and corporate responsibility continue to convey the idea that every sector of American life has something badly wrong with it. They continue to illustrate that the way to get one's way is to make a lot of assertive noises which shame and embarrass adversaries. Even the pages of such Establishment business magazines as *Fortune* and *Business Week* are filled with critical commentaries on their own subscribers, devoid now of gentle euphemism and sacred-cow restraints. Such journalism has brought far better results than bombs, damage to welfare offices, or traffic disruptions in Washington ever did.

To predict whether the New Third Sector and its tactics will survive is to invite dispute. Recent years have taught us the risks of social prediction. When President Nixon took office in 1968, he was ritually opposed to communism, government controls, deficit spending, and permissive law enforcement. In four years he was drinking toasts in Peking, imposing wage and price controls at home, running the largest budget deficit in United States history, and going to great, if temporary, lengths to protect his own staff from the Watergate incriminations. In the 1950s we agonized over the terrible spectacle of our children transfixed lethargically before the television set, not a thought in their autistic heads. By the end of the 1960s they were making revolutions. In 1959 the reigning topic in the nation's more thoughtful journals was adjusting to the fact of an affluent society. Ten years later, when the gross national product had expanded nearly 50 percent, the reigning topic centered on the agonies of poverty.

Still, the survival of the confrontational mode of the New Third Sector seems assured. It works too well not to attract new practitioners. And the world is too imperfect not to require new reforms.

Jean-François Revel argues that the groups I have called the New Third Sector, and their tactics, are indeed producing an American revolution, but that it will turn out to be a tolerable and beneficent revolution.[3] The nation will survive the temporary storm. Revel maintains that the success of a revolution depends on the economic strength and social vitality of the particular nation. The United States, he asserts, has the vitality

---

[3] See Jean-François Revel, *Without Marx or Jesus: The New American Revolution Has Begun*. Translated by Jack Bernard. New York: Doubleday, 1971.

and strength to survive the profound tremors that are shaking it. He acknowledges the possibility that society may crack under the strain of the dissenters who employ force and the protesters who use "revolutionary judo" to circumvent due process of law. But, he maintains, America will survive its own beneficial transformation because the industrial machine will be kept running. The population has always kept going day-to-day, attending to its normal tasks, even when it was badly alienated or aggravated or disturbed. Unlike the French or Italians, Americans do not translate their personal frustrations and discontents into general strikes that stop everything. They do not turn out the existing government in a sudden fit of anger or disgust. Americans separate work and politics into tight compartments. They keep going under the worst of circumstances. They have an enormous capacity to live simultaneously—and with little strain—in the multiple worlds of work, play, family, politics, and fantasy. The very insularity of the population's purposes, Revel suggests, reinforced by the pragmatism of its social attitudes, is precisely what holds it together through thick and thin.

This has certainly been so in the past, but the success of the New Third Sector's numerous groups in recent years portends the continuing presence of such groups in magnitudes and styles America has never before experienced. This, we have seen, creates the possibility of a serious erosion of the old consolidating virtues and ethics.

Nobody can deny that the New Third Sector has helped solve at least some of our problems. It has helped awaken the American people to long-ignored problems and injustices in their society, and to the possibility that they themselves can achieve results through new types of volunteer actions. With the persistent presence of continued, effective agitation, the population may in time be diverted from its more pressing private concerns. It may either be driven cynically to "get mine" or desperately to "get" the agitators.

The vociferous New Third Sector has been not only the irritated voice of the people but also their conscience. Although its main function has been to criticize business, government, and various other institutions, as well as a vast assortment of allegedly unfair, unjust, and corrupt conditions and practices in our society, the fact is that millions of people in business and government have also been aroused. Public and private bureaucracies have been forced to respond, and the society at large has become concerned with the very issues propounded by the activist organizations it so often dislikes.

Furthermore, people have been taught by the New Third Sector that it is possible to influence the world around them in ways never before contemplated. The Vietnam war is a good example. For four years between 1968 and 1972, polls persistently indicated that most people wanted the war to end. It dragged on through all those years, with only desultory objections, partly because some progress seemed afoot. The war seemed, at least, to be winding down, and the polls showed that the population generally felt that the President was doing his best finally to end it. He did in 1973. The President had indeed responded, or so most people felt. For many Americans this was welcome reassurance that they were not completely the helpless pawns of powerful forces, institutions, and politicians. Now that it is more moderate in its rhetoric and tactics, the New Third Sector may be restoring to the people a sense of control over their own destinies.

Americans have also learned a great deal from watching the participants in the New Third Sector. President Nixon himself proved his unintentional prowess as a revolutionary by publishing in 1970 the idea of the silent majority. The majority of Americans have been both silent and passive politically. By asking them now to speak out and openly oppose their adversaries, and by unleashing Vice President Agnew's own brand of vituperative rhetoric, he legitimized some New Third Sector ideas. Noisy assertiveness became an appropriate and acceptable form of social discourse, openly approved and encouraged by the man in the White House. The silent majority was represented as the virtuous majority. It was told to affirm its virtues not by silence but by the same mode of noisy activism that characterized its enemies.

The New Third Sector has, with the President's blessing, inadvertently provided the silent majority with visibility for its own views and causes, as well as a model for getting things done. Suddenly, the silent majority abandoned its silence. Assertive rhetoric, demonstrations, and boycotts became middle-class virtues.

But perhaps the most important of the New Third Sector's achievements is the fact that it has compelled people to recognize that neither business nor government, left alone, will alleviate their problems or frustrations. They have been forced to see that buck-passing is not the answer. In short, you have to get "involved."

Even the modern corporation—the most significant institution of American society—now clearly appreciates this necessity. It has come a long way. Business today is conducted in a much more open and responsible fashion than it was in the old robber-baron, public-be-damned days. In fact, we have today a swelling wave of corporate self-consciousness about the social role of business. For a while it even looked like the idea of corporate responsibility might actually be institutionalized, when President Nixon ceremoniously announced a plan to set up federally supported programs under which corporations would "solve" public sector problems. Though little came of it, the sentiment suggested a new view of the combined roles of business and government in public affairs. More particularly, it created an approved visibility for "getting involved" in matters that others had brought to the surface for our attention.

But everywhere we see hints of how unworkable Nixon's "solution" is likely to be. Superficially, prospects of success are good. At the higher levels in large corporations, executives generally applaud the idea that business can solve public problems and assert that business will do its part. Indeed, some of them assert that business will do more than its part, because government can do so little. On June 8, 1970, in a speech at the World Congress of Advertising in New York City, Dan Seymour, head of the J. Walter Thompson advertising agency, confidently declared:

> Let us make no mistake about it . . . it will be business that feeds the world, and depollutes the world and works out the system that will support life somehow among the fearsome mistakes the politicians make in each generation. It has to be business because we know governments can't do much about anything.

Its fatuousness aside, this argument runs that what individual businesses cannot do by themselves, they will do cooperatively through such ventures as the National Urban Coalition, the National Alliance of Businessmen, and various local groups. So runs the rhetoric—the rhetoric which promises not only that business can and will act socially responsible, and that society can count on that promise, but also that business will finally do what government and others cannot.

But the contradictions between word and deed, between affirmations and applications, have been legion. Contrary to what the New Third Sector shrilly declares, these contradictions have little to do with individual malevolence or greed. The simple fact is that public service is not a viable or dependable product of the business corporation. Nobody should be surprised that in such important areas as race relations and civil liberties our large companies have failed to take any significant initiative. They have often responded, after persistent pressures, but seldom led. Their presidents are not philosopher kings, nor can they be. Their speeches and public relations positions notwithstanding, they are still in the business of making money. In the crunch, public service necessarily comes last.

The following examples show the way business typically behaves when it is challenged to be responsive. The stories are not unusual; hundreds of similar ones could be told, in areas equally important to American society.

IMPORTS AND EXPORTS

As chairman of the board of E. I. du Pont de Nemours & Company, in the fall of 1965 Crawford Greenewalt published an article in *Dun's Review* saying in part that "industrial leaders can no longer insulate themselves from public affairs or consider their responsibilities as dealing solely with the profit-and-loss position of their enterprises." He said that corporations must "accept responsibility at the highest levels of national policy."

On March 20, 1970, Charles McCoy, the president. of Du Pont, told the annual meeting of the American Textile Manufacturers Institute in San Francisco that Du Pont would support the Institute's attempt to obtain legislation to control textile imports, especially from Japan. This was at the very time when the State Department was trying to build up Japan as America's political buffer in Asia.

Du Pont is the world's largest producer of man-made fibers. At the time of McCoy's speech, U.S. consumption of man-made fiber products was expected to rise from 10 billion pounds in 1969 to over 15 billion pounds by 1980. In 1969, imports had accounted for between 8 percent and 10 percent of U.S. consumption. Japan was responsible for around 40 percent of these imports, or between 3 percent and 4 percent of total U.S. consumption. McCoy said the Japanese were a threat and he was "disappointed and disillusioned" by the ineffectiveness of the voluntary import restraints that the government had urged on Japanese exporters. So, said McCoy, law or other persuasions had to be resorted to.

Certainly this 3 or 4 percent was no real threat to the $3.6 billion Du Pont company. But Du Pont had to go on record as opposing the growth of these imports lest its own fiber customers switch to competing domestic suppliers who supported restrictions. Thus, in spite of Crawford Greenewalt's selfless declaration about companies no longer being able to "consider their responsibilities as dealing solely with the profit-and-loss position of their enterprises," Du Pont took a strictly profit-and-loss-oriented action.

At the time of his *Dun's Review* article, Greenewalt was a signatory of the April 29, 1965, "Report to the President of the Special Committee on U.S. Trade Relations with East European Countries and the Soviet Union." The report advocated trading with "nations with whom we find frequent hostility," especially Communist nations, saying that such trade "can influence the internal development and the external policies of the European Communist societies along paths favorable to our purpose and world peace."

Also on the committee with Greenewalt were William Blackie, president of Caterpillar Tractor Company, and William Hewitt, chairman of the board of Deere & Company, both big steel users. Scarcely a month after the report was issued, the U.S. State Department announced that a unique arrangement had been worked out with the Japanese Iron and Steel Exporters Association, which represented Japan's nine biggest steel companies. In response to heavy pressure from American steel manufacturers, the Association had agreed that its members would hold their exports to the United States to 5.5 million metric tons in the ensuing year.

At that time, the United States officially viewed Japan as the strongest national force against Communist expansion in the Orient. President Nixon, in fact, had appointed a commission whose objective was to help keep Japan economically strong. Steel exports to the United States would do just that. Yet no dissenting word came from Mr. Blackie or Mr. Hewitt, or from their companies, Caterpillar and Deere. Apparently it is only in theory that American companies welcome the price-reducing effects of competition, and only in theory—and for public bamboozlement—that they advocate measures which are costly to themselves but beneficial for the nation.

In 1968 the *Harvard Business Review* ran an article called "Business Leadership and a Creative Society." [4] Its author was one of the most thoughtful and socially minded men in American business, Abram T. Collier, then president of New England Mutual Life Insurance Company. Collier wrote that "Business is not 'just business.' We must subject our old concepts of right and wrong, of good and bad, to a radical change." Business, he said, must abandon purely business-oriented values and adopt a body of venerable values that are found in all religions—service, goodness, fairness, and humility.

Just six months later, a well-known insurance company right down the street from Collier's Boston office canceled its liability and fire insurance coverage of the Arlington Street Church because the church had provided sanctuary for draft resisters. It was a widely publicized event. Yet not a single word of condemnation was to be heard from Mr. Collier or anybody else in the industry. In fact, that summer cancellations popped up all over the land, like measles in kindergarten. In Detroit over 300 property insurance policies were canceled. The St. Louis Housing Authority reported that it had been notified of cancellations of $52.4 million worth of coverage on five public housing projects, despite the fact

[4] *Harvard Business Review*, May 1968, p. 154ff.

that its contract with the insurance company had nearly two years to run. In this case the devastation of urban riots was the indicated reason.[5] Where, one is compelled to ask, were the industry spokesmen for such ideas as service, goodness, and fairness?

MINORITY-GROUP OPPORTUNITIES

In March 1968, when the devastating urban riots of the previous summer were still fresh in everyone's mind, President Johnson got the volunteer members of the National Alliance of Businessmen to try to line up summer jobs for high school ghetto youths—to get them off the streets and provide some hope and income. Supporting the program, Richard Chilcott, of the Nationwide Life Insurance Company of Columbus, Ohio, said: "Businessmen complain about how costly it is to bring in unskilled people just for the summer, but a riot is a lot more expensive." The NAB promised to line up 200,000 jobs.

By July 1968 only 120,000 jobs had been pledged, and only 27,000 youths were actually at work. Said a Milwaukee electrical equipment maker: "You just can't take on people for summer work when you're already laying people off." Said a San Francisco executive after hiring some of the youths: "We needed those new youngsters like a hole in the head." Good intentions succumbed to bad economic conditions.

---

[5] Such devastation was indeed costly. In one outbreak, the American Insurance Association reported $24 million of losses in Washington, D.C. alone.

A similar fate overtook related programs. In October 1969, Secretary of Commerce Maurice Stans enthusiastically publicized the names of 18 large companies that had agreed to set up investment funds to finance minority-group businessmen under a program optimistically called Project Enterprise. Each firm was to put up $150,000, and the federal government had pledged to match each dollar with another two of its own. In eight months, Stans said, 100 more companies would probably have signed up. But eight months later, in June 1970, only nine companies had kept their $150,000 pledge, and none of these had made any of the so-called black capitalism loans Stans had promised. Rocco Siciliano, the Deputy Secretary of Commerce, said: "It's hard to imbue businessmen with social consciousness when business is bad."

JOBS, the highly publicized hard-core-unemployment program, fared no better. It, too, enlisted business to help solve a serious public problem. The program, under another title, was first inaugurated in 1968 by President Johnson. It was one of the few Johnson programs that President Nixon embraced with anything resembling enthusiasm. Here was a perfect example of reliance on the private sector to get minority-group members started so they could eventually rely on themselves. The effort was widely publicized as the JOBS program—Job Opportunities in the Business Sector.

On May 14, 1969, the Chrysler Corporation contracted—with considerable fanfare—to "deliver 4,450 jobs" to the hard-core unemployed. Chrysler's public relations machinery helped get the agreement with the federal government all over Detroit's front pages. Buried deep in the publicity release was the fact that for this selfless deed Chrysler was to get $13.8 million from the federal government. But only ten months later, the $13.8 million notwithstanding, the Chrysler–Washington contract was quietly canceled "by mutual agreement." The reason was the auto-industry slump and widespread lay-offs. There is no record of any stockholders insisting that Chrysler, in spite of its galloping deficits, should discharge its social responsibilities by continuing the JOBS contract.

Nor did people pay much attention to an interesting related fact: Lynn Townsend, Chrysler's chairman of the board and chief executive officer, was slated to take over as chairman of the National Alliance of Businessmen just a few days after Chrysler's cancellation. NAB, of course, was the very businessmen's organization whose job it was to get companies to participate in the JOBS program from which Chrysler was withdrawing. Practical men of affairs, making practical separations between hard-headed economics and voluntary social service, failed to note any contradictions in Townsend's actions that week.

Given the choice between social responsibility and efficient performance, it is the nature of business to opt for the latter. In view of this inescapable fact of business life, one might expect businessmen at least to cease their hypocritical practice of preaching a goodness that they cannot fully deliver, that they will be forced willy-nilly to contradict in practice, and that, in any case, is usually a limited, parochial view of goodness. Business does some things superbly; others, not well at all. As the editors of *Fortune* magazine pointed out:

> It is only a slight exaggeration to state that American business, given the right incentives and conditions, can respond to almost any quantitative challenge. More goods, services, profits, factories, investments, sales effort—if demand presses, business will produce. . . . Change the discipline, introduce purposes linked to broad public responsibilities, however praiseworthy they may be, blur the criterion of performance, and the result is likely to be confusion and lack of sure-footedness. Such a shift in ground rules may throw the business community—and the country—into a spin.

Businessmen cannot reasonably be expected to don the aristocratic mantle of social responsibility, to do all the good deeds that need doing. As people's social and economic expectations rise, and their demands for more equity and amenities expand, one is tempted to suggest that business may have to abandon its historic reflexive opposition to the expansion of the state's powers and duties. Business' own self-interest may be best served not by minimizing the state, but by allowing its judicious expansion; not by fighting the state, but by helping it grow into an effective instrument of social management. This may be the only way business will ever become free to do what it does so well: respond efficiently and unselfconsciously to marketplace pressures and incentives.

But we have seen that government has its own bureaucratic rigidities and failings. The government's fumbling efforts to deal with such problems as poverty, crime, and minority-group discrimination lead one to doubt government's competence as much as business' reliability. It may be that in some crude fashion we shall have to accept the imperfections of all institutions, merely invoking the ancient sentiments of morality, civility, and community that in time guide men of power and influence to more salutory and responsive modes of behavior.

The search for solutions and answers has also raised the suggestion of collective decision making. George Cabot Lodge of Harvard University argues that the historic concept of the large corporation, for example, is obsolete, and that most big companies are becoming increasingly if uneasily aware of this. Lodge suggests that the large corporation is now actually a "community" rather than merely a private economic institution. It is a community of interests—managers, workers, stockholders, customers, citizens—and all these "interests" should therefore participate regularly in the collective decisions that collectively affect them. Many decisions that impinge heavily on all our lives can no longer be allowed to be totally private—or even, for that matter, totally "public," in the sense of their being made by government agencies alone.

The prototype of such decision-making machinery

can be seen on college campuses where faculty, staff, students, and members of the wider community in which the university is located are beginning to participate in major decisions on physical expansion, local housing, curriculum, admissions, and grades. The advocates of this kind of collective decision making assert that it does more than merely assure the consideration of a wide variety of viewpoints and interests. They argue that it is the administrative essence of responsiveness. They feel, moreover, that achieving responsiveness on the bigger issues will automatically eliminate much of the noisy outrage that has been employed so dramatically and divisively to command attention. The smaller, day-to-day problems of unresponsiveness will seem less obnoxious and will get gradually solved through the development of subsidiary machinery—much as when labor and management developed formal grievance procedures to handle day-to-day problems following the rise of collective bargaining on larger matters.

The major problem with this scenario is that in reality not everybody can participate in the decision-making process, though everybody is affected by it. Limited participation is a procedural necessity for all social and institutional decision making. There are just too many affected people and groups to accommodate them all in the decision-making process. Given this limitation, it seems logical to grant representation to the interest groups that are directly affected—customers, labor, stockholders, local communities, federal authorities, and ordinary citizens of the neighborhood. What, then, is the role of the New Third Sector groups—which are simply interested groups, not interest groups? Certainly representation should not be restricted to interest groups that gather collectively, as in a syndicalist state, to take care only of the interests they see for themselves and for each other. If there is to be representation it must be broader, but it is difficult to know where to draw the line.

It is also difficult to imagine how collective decision making would work in industry, and especially in government. Northeast Utilities, a holding company for several New England electric utilities, was involved in something of a collective effort for over a year in connection with the location of a new generating plant. The company even gave a citizens' group $180,000 to make engineering and other studies as to the pros and cons of building the plant in various locations. The money was given to the Boston Safe Deposit & Trust Company for disbursement on the understanding that the bank would act as a completely objective intermediary. It can be said that the process had some value; at least there was participation of the wider community where none had existed before. But four years later, as of mid-1973, the project was still in abeyance, thanks to the efforts of the citizens' group, whose members have opposed every suggested location on environmental and other grounds.

How long it will take to get any agreement may be judged by another utility's experience. New York City's Consolidated Edison Company was ineffectually involved in precisely the same hassle for nearly ten years in connection with the location of an atomic power generating plant. As a result, New York was perpetually plagued with electrical breakdowns and brownouts, and scorn was heaped on Con Ed for a "failure" that in reality represents the failure of the community to make a collective decision.

If neither business nor government nor special-interest groups can make our society more responsive, what can? We have come back full circle to the New Third Sector. The New Third Sector was born out of people's dissatisfactions with the institutions they created to serve them. It was made by people who came to the gradual, outraged conclusion that the institutions on which we depend to serve us served only themselves.

The fact that in these past years the nation has come alive to many of the New Third Sector's complaints and agitations may be a hopeful sign. It may mean that the New Third Sector's main bequest has been to revive in American society the concept of government by the people for the people. The silent majority has to some degree been jarred out of its apathy and feeling of helplessness by the vociferous New Third Sector tactics. Self-criticism has initially brought on a wave of national doubt and despair, but if the New Third Sector in the future adopts a more muted and constructive style (now that everyone seems more willing to listen), it is possible that new approaches and new hopes will be created, and concrete achievements will follow. This is at least as likely as stagnation, and more likely than chaos.

If this optimistic forecast is to materialize, the New Third Sector must also decide what concrete achievements to aim for. Its general goal is responsiveness, but how, exactly, is responsiveness to be defined in a highly bureaucratic society where bureaucracy is the inescapable consequence of the abundance people obviously want?

We make little progress if we define responsiveness abstractly. In these as in most matters, the utility of a definition resides in its guidance to practical action. Responsiveness is, therefore, all of the following: listening, meeting, sympathetic attitudes, good will, and some reasonable willingness to spend money for projects and programs aimed at correcting or alleviating the problems being talked about.

Obviously, nothing could sound more squishy to practical men of affairs than this "practical" definition. Yet responsiveness cannot possibly be achieved until all our organizations listen—to the extent that bureaucratic organizations can listen—with a third ear to the Third Sector noises that confront them. Members of the other two sectors, when confronted with agitators whose tactics may seem abhorrent, must try honestly to understand that few issues are clearly one-sided, and that they themselves generally see the world through rather foggy organizational prisms. Business and government must listen to the other view with patience and even sympathy, unless they want to risk the New Third Sector escalating its more dangerous tactics. Sometimes, when confronted with new symptoms of disorder, distortion, or aggravation, they must, under quiet circumstances, ask the clarifying questions themselves rather than waiting for agitators to ask them vociferously under noisy circumstances.

Responsiveness also requires "meeting," in the sense that people who have traditionally been on the outside of society's central decision-making processes should be met with and brought into the critical mainstream. Providing them with a genuine sense of identity and participation is a specific, and important, means of being responsive.

And it requires a greater willingness to spend money on the solution of salient social problems. We have seen—especially in the areas of urban renewal, low-income housing, youth employment, poverty programs, and business-subsidy projects—that money can be unwisely, wastefully, and corruptly spent. But for a time, spending money in these areas at least showed that government and the rest of society cared—that they were concerned with values other than those which could be expressed in the conventional cost-benefit analysis. Spending money palpably symbolizes a commitment to action that nothing else can so tangibly symbolize. That kind of spending is important precisely for its visible and costly character—and often justifiable for that reason alone. But it is also dangerous. It is easy to announce a massive budget for a good cause, and easy to receive credit for spending that may be predictably useless, or at least wasteful. Nevertheless, in times of stress and crisis it is better to err on the side of pointless spending than to invoke a quantitative calculation of efficiency. The latter will be interpreted as just more of the same heartless impersonality which created the stress and crisis in the first place. It is better, in such times, to have spent and failed economically than to have resisted and therefore failed socially and politically.

But all this still leaves any thoughtful person understandably uneasy. Does responsiveness mean a kind of soft-headed willingness to accommodate any kind of opposing group, regardless of its purpose or plans? Does it mean nothing but capitulation—nothing but giving in to all sorts of disorderly and irresponsible demands from noisy leaders with vest-pocket followings, leaders who, in any case, are not sensibly to be relied upon for either their analysis of society or their prescriptions for its improvement?

Obviously not. We need not listen to and meet with everybody—let alone capitulate to them. To do so would be to succumb to a malignancy as bad as the malignant conditions they complain about.

Responsiveness creates no obligation of instant or substantive accommodation to one's adversaries. But it does require the sensitive and constructive acknowledgment of their existence and acknowledgment of their claims at least to the extent of agreeing to talk about them. When people feel deeply that there is an injustice, and feel it strongly enough to create an inflammatory style of tactics or rhetoric, ignoring them simply worsens the disorder that has already begun. To firmly "stand on one's principles" is to ignore the future and what may be necessary for survival in the long run.

Discussion does not mean capitulation; agreeing to talk about an issue does not concede the legitimacy of either one's adversary or his accusations. It concedes only that society cannot function and survive unless everyone at least tries to do his part. If that means conferring with avowed enemies who have completely different values or who systematically distort the facts, then that may be a price worth paying to prevent disorder and disastrous dissonance. In such cases, one may have to listen not because of any faith that listening will produce new understanding, but rather because the claims and assertions being made (which to the listener are obviously disagreeable, silly, dangerous, or even lunatic) will in the process be shown for what they are and the agitation therefore modified or defused.

Clearly, there will always be people who will find it so distasteful to listen to or negotiate with those who are palpably "crazies"—groups who are high on their own discordant sounds and who make up with the virulence of their tactics what they lack in magnitude of following —that they will feel not only that it is fruitless to talk with these groups but also that engaging in discussion with them would in some fashion legitimize their claims. Why "listen" and "discuss" with them?

Actually, one needn't. If one has already listened to a particular group and has fairly and firmly decided that the group is "crazy" and lacks any serious constituency, then it is obviously silly to prescribe that one should do any further talking or negotiating with it. In that circumstance, however, it is also important not to fight. It is best to ignore, as was done so effectively with the sit-ins at the University of Chicago in 1970.

It is not a condition of responsiveness that one must be always and under all circumstances "responsive" in the fashion I have proposed. Times change. In some times, as in May 1970 (the Cambodian bombing and Kent State), there was such widespread and frustrated outrage among the young that to have actively resisted or ignored them would have worsened a rapidly worsening situation. Similarly, during the national meat boycott in April 1973, no conceivably useful advantage could have accrued to anyone by making an opposing public scene against the boycotters. Indeed, it would have been dysfunctional even to have told them that they might achieve (temporarily) the opposite of their intentions. There was simply too much sympathy for their complaints. In any case, the significance of the boycott lay in its political, not its economic, message. For the butchers, the meat packers, and the farmers, to say nothing was just the right thing. It was a political matter.

It is obviously important to be sensibly selective and understanding about the New Third Sector issues that seem daily to erupt. A general rule may be that the greater the number of people who seem involved with or touched by an issue, the greater the likelihood that some serious or fundamental grievance is being aired. To attack or oppose it without listening or discussion is to worsen the situation.

The trick for those in positions of power and responsibility is to make the appropriate distinctions between the spurious and the real, the transient and the lasting, the serious and the aberrant. To make these distinctions generally requires learning more, and often that can be done only by listening and discussing, even when it is distasteful. The posture to avoid is the out-of-hand assumption that nothing useful could conceivably be learned by trying to learn more about the issues being aired.

Lord Acton long ago observed that man sacrificed freedom in his search for impossible justice. Whether this is true or not, people continue to seek it. And if people in power refuse to yield an ear to the justice-seekers because they are disorderly and relatively powerless, they may find themselves in deep trouble. The opposite of Lord Acton's dictum also holds: Man may sacrifice order in the attempt to preserve impossible freedom.

St. Luke's prescription is more relevant: To those whom much is given, much is expected. Men of power and influence have a greater obligation to listen and respond precisely because their power and influence insulate them from the necessity to do so.

Despite the frequent myopia of men in power, and despite the frequently self-serving behavior of both the corporate and government worlds, a look at the total picture indicates that our society is by no means unresponsive. While this is little consolation for those caught in its less responsive networks, the plain truth is that in most respects America is probably more responsive than any society on the globe. England may have more generous public health services, but its public education is substantially less generous and its hereditary barriers to social mobility infinitely greater. Sweden may have its middle way, but it is a tightly confined middle that hampers flexible economic expansion and exploration of alternative social arrangements. France boasts democracy, but arrests of journalists critical of the state are not uncommon. When we get away from headlines and look closely at the lives of ordinary people, we find that many more socially benign things get done in America and people lead much more active, productive, and fulfilling lives than the fluent critics of America allege.

Given their sheer size, American institutions are remarkably responsive. The bureaucracies bend—perhaps slowly, but bend they do. The political system creaks slowly but ineluctably toward, not away from, its duty to solve the nation's problems. Society is not indifferent, only halting.

The hard truth seems to be that a complex industrial system cannot be made totally responsive. It can only be made less unresponsive. What may look like injustice, unfairness, or even callousness to outsiders are often simply the inescapable consequences of conflicting claims on resources, limited means, and the creaky procedures of a society whose creakiness is a direct result of its democraticness and its size. Responsiveness should not be defined in terms of what people can manage to get, and how fast they can get it, but in terms of the processes by which decisions and choices are made.

The New Third Sector needs to learn that many of the injustices and problems which it fulminates against—and which it so cavalierly blames on a sinister combination of greed and bias—are simply accidents. Social injustices are often the unintended outcomes of perfectly innocent individual choices. In the words of Thomas Schelling, there is a frequent divergence between what people are individually motivated to do and what they might like to accomplish together. Individuals would rather drive their cars to work than take a bus, but still they want to eradicate carbon monoxide pollution. People want to vacation in Yosemite, but don't want it crowded and cluttered and don't want the little seedlings trampled. The fact that seedlings get trampled does not prove that the individual tramplers are indifferent or selfish. Accidents happen. Other things occupy their minds as they walk about. Nor is it particularly helpful to accuse legislators and government administrators of diabolism for their failure to create more public parks, or to blame business for the scarcity of seedlings because businesses grow lumber for profit.

This is not to imply that once injustices are exposed there is any longer an excuse for indifference. But in social affairs, as in physics, perfection is impossible. The physicist cannot produce a perfect vacuum. The politician cannot produce a perfect society. It is impossible to get agreement as to what social perfection might be. There can be no perfect justice, perfect fairness, or perfect responsiveness. A hermit lives alone, giving no quarter to anyone, save nature. When we live among each other—when we have a "society"—we are compelled to compromise our individual wills and wishes. The best society is not one in which the sum total of these compromises is least. It is simply one in which our most valued wills and wishes are least compromised. We will tolerate a great many policemen on the streets telling us whether to stop or go, but not a single one in our homes telling us whether to leave or stay.

Since society is by nature a complex compromise of its inhabitants, as things change some will believe that the compromises they are making are disproportionately high—that there is inequity and therefore injustice. They will also feel that society's mechanisms for dealing with injustices have gotten rigidly institutionalized, often at the expense of the weak and for the profit of the strong. That feeling is likely to generate a fairly strong reaction. Thus in every society, save a totally static one, there will always be those who feel exploited or unfairly treated. Whether they are completely justified is a separate question. Arguing that their facts are wrong or their reasoning faulty doesn't even have the utility of a diversionary tactic. The point is that when feelings of injustice and wrongdoing are strong and prevalent, they can, under the right conditions, escalate into a major social disorder.

In recent years, conditions in America have been hospitable to that escalation. And people in positions of power, even if they were irreconcilably opposed to their critics or opponents, found that when the rhetoric reached a high decibel level they had no sensible choice but to engage them in discussion. The critical question is when to decide to talk. Is the issue real or spurious? Is the constituency real or manufactured? Is it a brief and trivial exception, or a serious and lasting condition? In a specific situation, how long should one wait before officially recognizing one's adversaries and responding to them?

In the period between 1963 and 1970 Americans often waited too long. They let discontents escalate to a point where meliorating and productive discussion was no longer possible. In those years, the whole society often became so inflamed and exacerbated that it seemed to be risking its own stability. Too many organizations and officials had become obsessively and defensively insular, preoccupied with operational efficiency rather than with overall effectiveness. Social and human consequences not normally recorded in profit-and-loss statements, balance sheets, or cost-benefit calculations were, in keeping with traditional practice, ignored. These issues continued to be disregarded in spite of rising public insistence that they be not only recognized but constructively dealt with.

When responses were finally forthcoming, it was in an atmosphere of such profound inflammation, cynicism, and despair that effective talk and reasonable solutions were almost impossible. Some reasonable progress was made after the violent rhetoric died down as a consequence of the fragmentation and exhaustion of the most inflamed of the New Third Sector groups, but for a time

America teetered dangerously on the brink of tearing itself to pieces.

The question for every organization, bureau, department, manager, politician, or functionary is how and when to listen and to what—how to perform efficiently and well by standards not accounted for in the traditional financial calculus of business or the vote-getting calculus of politics. Serious suggestions for ways of accounting for these "externalities" have been made by two Harvard Business School professors, Raymond A. Bauer and Dann H. Fenn, Jr.,[6] and by the British management consultant John Humble.[7] Both describe, and Humble shows in specific operating detail, how firms might install a system for auditing and measuring their social performance just as they now audit and measure their economic performance. It is a good start. But while economic performance can be quantitatively metricized in a profit-and-loss statement, it is questionable whether an individual firm's social performance can be equally metricized. Indeed, the risk is that an effort will be made to do just that, thus once again reducing to cold, quantitative calculation precisely the things that many people believe require a more humane attitude. There is also a risk of limiting to consideration only those things that are readily quantifiable. The Humble proposal avoids both of these traps. It tries

---

[6] *The Corporate Social Audit.* New York: Russell Sage Foundation, 1972.

[7] *Social Responsibility Audit.* London: Foundation for Business Responsibility, 1973. (American edition: AMA, 1973.)

to capture in its more qualitative auditing screen even the plight of Kafkaesque characters caught in the serpentine nexus of bureaucratic processes.

A regular, self-administered social audit can have value. If adopted in whole or in part it can institutionalize (yes, bureaucratize!) a procedure of self-surveillance. And even though this form of self-surveillence suffers from the fact of its being conducted by insiders whose perceptions will be conditioned by their insidedness, it at least creates the necessity of organizational narcissism. Of course, outsiders can be enlisted in the task. In either case, the organization must look at its deeds and consequences in areas not usually, or at least not formally, looked at before. To be made, by the system, to look is to be made aware—albeit by a bureaucratic device—of the consequences of one's own persistent bureaucratic mode. The social audit may therefore make the organization routinely sensitive to consequences it never before either deemed to exist or acknowledged any responsibility for.

But it will take a great deal of effort and advocacy to make the audit work and keep it going. Things that lie outside the direct operating purposes and interests of the organization seldom command the sustained interest and attention of men whose effectiveness is, in the end, measured on scales relating inescapably to the organization's inside purposes. The demand for efficiency in the execution of the organization's principal task can seldom be compromised by pleading attention to peripheral tasks.

Commitment to responsiveness does not require abandonment of efficiency—only some socially functional redefinition of its meaning. Nor does it require abandonment of toughness and thoroughness. A responsive and loving parent is not necessarily an indulgent or permissive parent. It is possible to be both indulgent and firm, depending on the circumstances. Adults in organizations know as well as children in families that different situations justify different modes of behavior. They also know, or should know, that if firmness goes unexplicated —if the possibility of discussion is denied—then firmness looks (and indeed is) arbitrary. The reaction will be correspondingly arbitrary, and therefore socially malignant.

The tough and disequilibrating tactics of the New Third Sector organizations have not been historic accidents, springing irrationally from nothing and going nowhere. They sprang from irrationalities and injustices —some just perceived as such, others real. It is important to understand their origins and purposes in order to recognize the urgency of the problems that they have been highlighting for our attention. We need not condone their tactics in order to understand their reasons for using them. We need not agree with their claims and accusations in order to accept the underlying necessity to create a more responsive and benign society. As we accept this necessity we move toward it.

What is now required is some balance and restraint in the way we describe our failings and handle our self-improvement. I have said that our society simply cannot stand all the one-sided, accusatory rhetoric to which it is being so relentlessly subjected. Neither can it stand the opposing aberration: euphoric idealization of everything that is right in America, a retreat to lofty Fourth-of-July platitudes that speak in glorious abstractions about a past that never was.

Faith in the principles of our historic fathers is an empty sham when not harnessed to purposeful actions. When government and business do not take these actions —when bureaucracy and self-interest and timidity cover up our most terrible problems and actively delay their urgent solution—it is not surprising that somebody blows the whistle. The New Third Sector has been that somebody. But its whistle has been an abrasive siren that itself damages the public's capacity to hear and effectively respond.

Still, the social voluntarism that the New Third Sector represents has turned out to be a powerful engine for change. The New Third Sector is not an alternative to electoral politics or formal government or genuinely responsive attitudes of people in positions of power. It is, rather, complementary to these things, even when its excesses threaten the stability of the society itself. If society wants to protect itself against the excesses of the New Third Sector, it must cope with some of the terrible problems that gave rise to it. It must be responsive, in both small and large things, through electoral politics and committed personal attitudes.

The patience of the past, which assumed that in due time the right things would somehow finally happen by themselves, no longer works. Now some are impatiently asking too much, in contrast to those who've asked too little, and society has no choice but to do what's right. It must use politics and all other cooperative means to achieve the kind of benign, responsive, and compassionate institutions without which society in any civilized sense is impossible and the alternatives unbearable.

INDEX